Little Rivers

by Henry van Dyke

I0427730

"And suppose he takes nothing, yet he enjoyeth a delightful walk by pleasant Rivers, in sweet Pastures, amongst odoriferous Flowers, which gratifie his Senses, and delight his Mind; which Contentments induce many (who affect not Angling) to choose those places of pleasure for their summer Recreation and Health."

COL. ROBERT VENABLES, The Experienc'd Angler, 1662.

DEDICATION

To one who wanders by my side As cheerfully as waters glide; Whose eyes are brown as woodland streams, And very fair and full of dreams; Whose heart is like a mountain spring, Whose thoughts like merry rivers sing: To her---my little daughter Brooke-- I dedicate this little book.

CONTENTS

PRELUDE

AN ANGLER'S WISH IN TOWN

When tulips bloom in Union Square, And timid breaths of vernal air Are wandering down the dusty town, Like children lost in Vanity Fair;

When every long, unlovely row Of westward houses stands aglow And leads the eyes toward sunset skies, Beyond the hills where green trees grow;

Then weary is the street parade, And weary books, and weary trade: I'm only wishing to go a-fishing; For this the month of May was made.

I guess the pussy-willows now Are creeping out on every bough Along the brook; and robins look For early worms behind the plough.

The thistle-birds have changed their dun For yellow coats to match the sun; And in the same array of flame The Dandelion Show's begun.

The flocks of young anemones Are dancing round the budding trees: Who can help wishing to go a-fishing In days as full of joy as these?

I think the meadow-lark's clear sound Leaks upward slowly from the ground, While on the wing the bluebirds ring Their wedding-bells to woods around:

The flirting chewink calls his dear Behind the bush; and very near, Where water flows, where green grass grows, Song-sparrows gently sing, "Good cheer:"

And, best of all, through twilight's calm The hermit-thrush repeats his psalm: How much I'm wishing to go a-fishing In days so sweet with music's balm!

'Tis not a proud desire of mine; I ask for nothing superfine; No heavy weight, no salmon great, To break the record, or my line:

Only an idle little stream, Whose amber waters softly gleam, Where I may wade, through woodland shade, And cast the fly, and loaf, and dream:

Only a trout or two, to dart From foaming pools, and try my art: No more I'm wishing--old-fashioned fishing, And just a day on Nature's heart.

1894.

LITTLE RIVERS

A river is the most human and companionable of all inanimate things. It has a life, a character, a voice of its own, and is as full of good fellowship as a sugar-maple is of sap. It can talk in various tones, loud or low, and of many subjects, grave and gay. Under favourable circumstances it will even make a shift to sing, not in a fashion that can be reduced to notes and set down in black and white on a sheet of paper, but in a vague, refreshing manner, and to a wandering air that goes

"Over the hills and far away."

For real company and friendship, there is nothing outside of the animal kingdom that is comparable to a river.

I will admit that a very good case can be made out in favour of some other objects of natural affection. For example, a fair apology has been offered by those ambitious persons who have fallen in love with the sea. But, after all, that is a formless and disquieting passion. It lacks solid comfort and mutual confidence. The sea is too big for loving, and too uncertain. It will not fit into our thoughts. It has no personality because it has so many. It is a salt abstraction. You might as well think of loving a glittering generality like "the American woman." One would be more to the purpose.

Mountains are more satisfying because they are more individual. It is possible to feel a very strong attachment for a certain range whose outline has grown familiar to our eyes, or a clear peak that has looked down, day after day, upon our joys and sorrows, moderating our passions with its calm aspect. We come back from our travels, and the sight of such a well-known mountain is like meeting an old friend unchanged. But it is a one-sided affection. The mountain is voiceless and imperturbable; and its very loftiness and serenity sometimes make us the more lonely.

Trees seem to come closer to our life. They are often rooted in our richest feelings, and our sweetest memories, like birds, build nests in their branches. I remember, the last time that I saw James Russell Lowell, (only a few weeks before his musical voice was hushed,) he walked out with me into the quiet garden at Elmwood to say good-bye. There was a great horse-chestnut tree beside the house, towering above the gable, and covered with blossoms from base to summit,--a pyramid of green supporting a thousand smaller pyramids of white. The poet looked up at it with his gray, pain- furrowed face, and laid his trembling hand upon the trunk. "I planted the nut," said he, "from which this tree grew. And my father was with me and showed me how to plant it."

Yes, there is a good deal to be said in behalf of tree-worship; and when I recline with my friend Tityrus beneath the shade of his favourite oak, I consent in his devotions. But when I invite him with me to share my orisons, or wander alone to indulge the luxury of grateful, unlaborious thought, my feet turn not to a tree, but to the bank of a river, for there the musings of solitude find a friendly accompaniment, and human intercourse is purified and sweetened by the flowing, murmuring water. It is by a river that I would choose to make love, and to revive old friendships, and to play with the children, and to confess my faults, and to escape from vain, selfish desires, and to cleanse my mind from all the false and foolish things that mar the joy and peace of living. Like David's hart, I pant for the water-brooks. There is wisdom in the advice of Seneca, who says, "Where a spring rises, or a river flows, there should we build altars and offer sacrifices."

The personality of a river is not to be found in its water, nor in its bed, nor in its shore. Either of these elements, by itself, would be nothing. Confine the fluid contents of the noblest stream in a walled channel of stone, and it ceases to be a stream; it becomes what Charles Lamb calls "a mockery of a river--a liquid artifice--a wretched conduit." But take away the water from the most beautiful river-banks, and what is left? An ugly road with none to travel it; a long, ghastly scar on the bosom of the earth.

The life of a river, like that of a human being, consists in the union of soul and body, the water and the banks. They belong together. They act and react upon each other. The stream moulds and makes the shore; hollowing out a bay here, and building a long point there; alluring the little bushes close to its side, and bending the tall slim trees over its current; sweeping a rocky ledge clean of everything but moss, and sending a still lagoon full of white arrow-heads and rosy knot-weed far back into the meadow. The shore guides and controls the stream; now detaining and now advancing it; now bending it in a hundred sinuous curves, and now speeding it straight as a wild-bee on its homeward flight; here hiding the water in a deep cleft overhung with green branches, and there spreading it out, like a mirror framed in daisies, to reflect the sky and the clouds; sometimes breaking it with sudden turns and unexpected falls into a foam of musical laughter, sometimes soothing it into a sleepy motion like the flow of a dream.

Is it otherwise with the men and women whom we know and like? Does not the spirit influence the form, and the form affect the spirit? Can we divide and separate them in our affections?

I am no friend to purely psychological attachments. In some unknown future they may be satisfying, but in the present I want your words and your voice with your thoughts, your looks and your gestures to interpret your feelings. The warm, strong grasp of Greatheart's hand is as dear to me as the steadfast fashion of his friendships; the lively, sparkling eyes of the master of Rudder Grange charm me as much as the nimbleness of his fancy; and the firm poise of the Hoosier Schoolmaster's shaggy head gives me new confidence in the solidity of his views of life. I like the pure tranquillity of Isabel's brow as well as her

"most silver flow Of subtle-paced counsel in distress."

The soft cadences and turns in my lady Katrina's speech draw me into the humour of her gentle judgments of men and things. The touches of quaintness in Angelica's dress, her folded kerchief and smooth-parted hair, seem to partake of herself, and enhance my admiration for the sweet order of her thoughts and her old- fashioned ideals of love and duty. Even so the stream and its channel are one life, and I cannot think of the swift, brown flood of the Batiscan without its shadowing primeval forests, or the crystalline current of the Boquet without its beds of pebbles and golden sand and grassy banks embroidered with flowers.

Every country--or at least every country that is fit for habitation--has its own rivers; and every river has its own quality; and it is the part of wisdom to know and love as many as you can, seeing each in the fairest possible light, and receiving from each the best that it has to give. The torrents of Norway leap down from their mountain home with plentiful cataracts, and run brief but glorious races to the sea. The streams of England move smoothly through green fields and beside ancient, sleepy towns. The Scotch rivers brawl through the open moorland and flash along steep Highland glens. The rivers of the Alps are born in icy caves, from which they issue forth with furious, turbid waters; but when their anger has been forgotten in the slumber of some blue lake, they flow down more softly to see the vineyards of France and Italy, the gray castles of Germany, the verdant meadows of Holland. The mighty rivers of the West roll their yellow floods through broad valleys, or plunge down dark canyons. The rivers of the South creep under dim arboreal archways hung with banners of waving moss. The Delaware and the Hudson and the Connecticut are the children of the Catskills and the Adirondacks and the White Mountains, cradled among the forests of spruce and hemlock, playing through a wild woodland youth, gathering strength from numberless tributaries to bear their great burdens of lumber and turn the wheels of many mills, issuing from the hills to water a thousand farms, and descending at last, beside new cities, to the ancient sea.

Every river that flows is good, and has something worthy to be loved. But those that we love most are always the ones that we have known best,--the stream that ran before our father's door, the current on which we ventured our first boat or cast our first fly, the brook on whose banks we first picked the twinflower of young love. However far we may travel, we come back to Naaman's state of mind: "Are not Abana and Pharpar, rivers of Damascus, better than all the waters of Israel?"

It is with rivers as it is with people: the greatest are not always the most agreeable, nor the best to live with. Diogenes must have been an uncomfortable bedfellow: Antinous was bored to death in the society of the Emperor Hadrian: and you can imagine much better company for a walking trip than Napoleon Bonaparte. Semiramis was a lofty queen, but I fancy that Ninus had more than one bad quarter-of-an-hour with her: and in "the spacious times of great Elizabeth" there was many a milkmaid whom the wise man would have chosen for his friend, before the royal red-haired virgin. "I confess," says the poet Cowley, "I love littleness almost in all things. A little convenient Estate, a little chearful House, a little Company, and a very little

Feast, and if I were ever to fall in Love again, (which is a great Passion, and therefore, I hope, I have done with it,) it would be, I think, with Prettiness, rather than with Majestical Beauty. I would neither wish that my Mistress, nor my Fortune, should be a Bona Roba, as Homer uses to describe his Beauties, like a daughter of great Jupiter for the stateliness and largeness of her Person, but as Lucretius says:

'Parvula, pumilio, [Greek text omitted], tota merum sal.'"

Now in talking about women it is prudent to disguise a prejudice like this, in the security of a dead language, and to intrench it behind a fortress of reputable authority. But in lowlier and less dangerous matters, such as we are now concerned with, one may dare to speak in plain English. I am all for the little rivers. Let those who will, chant in heroic verse the renown of Amazon and Mississippi and Niagara, but my prose shall flow--or straggle along at such a pace as the prosaic muse may grant me to attain--in praise of Beaverkill and Neversink and Swiftwater, of Saranac and Raquette and Ausable, of Allegash and Aroostook and Moose River. "Whene'er I take my walks abroad," it shall be to trace the clear Rauma from its rise on the fjeld to its rest in the fjord; or to follow the Ericht and the Halladale through the heather. The Ziller and the Salzach shall be my guides through the Tyrol; the Rotha and the Dove shall lead me into the heart of England. My sacrificial flames shall be kindled with birch-bark along the wooded stillwaters of the Penobscot and the Peribonca, and my libations drawn from the pure current of the Ristigouche and the Ampersand, and my altar of remembrance shall rise upon the rocks beside the falls of Seboomok.

I will set my affections upon rivers that are not too great for intimacy. And if by chance any of these little ones have also become famous, like the Tweed and the Thames and the Arno, I at least will praise them, because they are still at heart little rivers.

If an open fire is, as Charles Dudley Warner says, the eye of a room; then surely a little river may be called the mouth, the most expressive feature, of a landscape. It animates and enlivens the whole scene. Even a railway journey becomes tolerable when the track follows the course of a running stream.

What charming glimpses you catch from the window as the train winds along the valley of the French Broad from Asheville, or climbs the southern Catskills beside the Aesopus, or slides down the Pusterthal with the Rienz, or follows the Glommen and the Gula from Christiania to Throndhjem. Here is a mill with its dripping, lazy wheel, the type of somnolent industry; and there is a white cascade, foaming in silent pantomime as the train clatters by; and here is a long, still pool with the cows standing knee-deep in the water and swinging their tails in calm indifference to the passing world; and there is a lone fisherman sitting upon a rock, rapt in contemplation of the point of his rod. For a moment you become a partner of his tranquil enterprise. You turn around, you crane your neck to get the last sight of his motionless angle. You do not know what kind of fish he expects to catch, nor what species of bait he is using, but at least you pray that he may have a bite before the train swings around the next curve. And if perchance your wish is granted, and you see him gravely draw some unknown, reluctant, shining reward of patience from the water, you feel like swinging your hat from the window and crying out "Good luck!"

Little rivers seem to have the indefinable quality that belongs to certain people in the world,--the power of drawing attention without courting it, the faculty of exciting interest by their very presence and way of doing things.

The most fascinating part of a city or town is that through which the water flows. Idlers always choose a bridge for their place of meditation when they can get it; and, failing that, you will find them sitting on the edge of a quay or embankment, with their feet hanging over the water. What a piquant mingling of indolence and vivacity you can enjoy by the river-side! The best point of view in Rome, to my taste, is the Ponte San Angelo; and in Florence or Pisa I never tire of loafing along the Lung' Arno. You do not know London until you have seen it from the Thames. And you will miss the charm of Cambridge unless you take a little boat and go drifting on the placid Cam, beneath the bending trees, along the backs of the colleges.

But the real way to know a little river is not to glance at it here or there in the course of a hasty journey, nor to become acquainted with it after it has been partly civilised and spoiled by too close contact with the works of man. You must go to its native haunts; you must see it in youth and freedom; you must accommodate yourself to its pace, and give yourself to its influence, and follow its meanderings whithersoever they may lead you.

Now, of this pleasant pastime there are three principal forms. You may go as a walker, taking the river-side path, or making a way for yourself through the tangled thickets or across the open meadows. You may go as a sailor, launching your light canoe on the swift current and committing yourself for a day, or a week, or a month, to the delightful uncertainties of a voyage through the forest. You may go as a wader, stepping into the stream and going down with it, through rapids and shallows and deeper pools, until you come to the end of your courage and the daylight. Of these three ways I know not which is best. But in all of them the essential thing is that you must be willing and glad to be led; you must take the little river for your guide, philosopher, and friend.

And what a good guidance it gives you. How cheerfully it lures you on into the secrets of field and wood, and brings you acquainted with the birds and the flowers. The stream can show you, better than any other teacher, how nature works her enchantments with colour and music.

Go out to the Beaver-kill

"In the tassel-time of spring,"

and follow its brimming waters through the budding forests, to that corner which we call the Painter's Camp. See how the banks are all enamelled with the pale hepatica, the painted trillium, and the delicate pink-veined spring beauty. A little later in the year, when the ferns are uncurling their long fronds, the troops of blue and white violets will come dancing down to the edge of the stream, and creep venturously out to the very end of that long, moss- covered log in the water. Before these have vanished, the yellow crow-foot and the cinquefoil will appear, followed by the star- grass and the loose-strife and the golden St. John's-wort. Then the unseen painter begins to mix the royal colour on his palette, and the red of the bee-balm catches your eye. If you are lucky, you may find, in midsummer, a slender fragrant spike of the purple- fringed orchis, and you cannot help finding the universal self- heal. Yellow returns in the drooping flowers of the jewel-weed, and blue repeats itself in the trembling hare-bells, and scarlet is glorified in the flaming robe of the cardinal-flower. Later still, the summer closes in a splendour of bloom, with gentians and asters and goldenrod.

You never get so close to the birds as when you are wading quietly down a little river, casting your fly deftly under the branches for the wary trout, but ever on the lookout for all the various pleasant things that nature has to bestow upon you. Here you shall come upon the cat-bird at her morning bath, and hear her sing, in a clump of pussy-willows, that low, tender, confidential song which she keeps for the hours of domestic intimacy. The spotted sandpiper will run along the stones before you, crying, "wet-feet, wet-feet!" and bowing and teetering in the friendliest manner, as if to show you the way to the best pools. In the thick branches of the hemlocks that stretch across the stream, the tiny warblers, dressed in a hundred colours, chirp and twitter confidingly above your head; and the Maryland yellow-throat, flitting through the bushes like a little gleam of sunlight, calls "witchery, witchery, witchery!" That plaintive, forsaken, persistent note, never ceasing, even in the noonday silence, comes from the wood-pewee, drooping upon the bough of some high tree, and complaining, like Mariana in the moated grange, "weary, weary, weary!"

When the stream runs out into the old clearing, or down through the pasture, you find other and livelier birds,--the robins, with his sharp, saucy call and breathless, merry warble; the bluebird, with his notes of pure gladness, and the oriole, with his wild, flexible whistle; the chewink, bustling about in the thicket, talking to his sweetheart in French, "cherie, cherie!" and the song-sparrow, perched on his favourite limb of a young maple, dose beside the water, and singing happily, through sunshine and through rain. This is the true bird of the brook, after all: the winged spirit of cheerfulness and contentment, the patron saint of little rivers, the fisherman's friend. He seems to enter into your sport with his good wishes, and for an hour at a time, while you are trying every fly in your book, from a black gnat to a white miller, to entice the crafty old trout at the foot of the meadow-pool, the song-sparrow, close above you, will be chanting patience and encouragement. And when at last success crowns your endeavour, and the parti-coloured prize is glittering in your net, the bird on the bough breaks out in an ecstasy of congratulation: "catch 'im, catch 'im, catch 'im; oh, what a pretty fellow! sweet!"

There are other birds that seem to have a very different temper. The blue-jay sits high up in the withered-pine tree, bobbing up and down, and calling to his mate in a tone of affected sweetness. "salute-her, salute-her," but when you come in sight he flies away with a harsh cry of "thief, thief, thief!" The kingfisher, ruffling his crest in solitary pride on the end of a dead branch, darts down the stream at your approach, winding up his red angrily as if he despised you for interrupting his fishing. And the cat- bird, that sang so charmingly while she thought herself unobserved, now tries to scare you away by screaming "snake, snake!"

As evening draws near, and the light beneath the trees grows yellower, and the air is full of filmy insects out for their last dance, the voice of the little river becomes louder and more distinct. The true poets have often noticed this apparent increase in the sound of flowing waters at nightfall. Gray, in one of his letters, speaks of "hearing the murmur of many waters not audible in the daytime." Wordsworth repeats the same thought almost in the same words:

"A soft and lulling sound is heard Of streams inaudible by day."

And Tennyson, in the valley of Cauteretz, tells of the river

"Deepening his voice with deepening of the night."

It is in this mystical hour that you will hear the most celestial and entrancing of all bird-notes, the songs of the thrushes,--the hermit, and the wood-thrush, and the veery. Sometimes, but not often, you will see the singers. I remember once, at the close of a beautiful day's fishing on the Swiftwater, I came out, just after sunset, into a little open space in an elbow of the stream. It was still early spring, and the leaves were tiny. On the top of a small sumac, not thirty feet away from me, sat a veery. I could see the pointed spots upon his breast, the swelling of his white throat, and the sparkle of his eyes, as he poured his whole heart into a long liquid chant, the clear notes rising and falling, echoing and interlacing in endless curves of sound,

"Orb within orb, intricate, wonderful."

Other bird-songs can be translated into words, but not this. There is no interpretation. It is music,--as Sidney Lanier defines it,--

"Love in search of a word."

But it is not only to the real life of birds and flowers that the little rivers introduce you. They lead you often into familiarity with human nature in undress, rejoicing in the liberty of old clothes, or of none at all. People do not mince along the banks of streams in patent-leather shoes or crepitating silks. Corduroy and home-spun and flannel are the stuffs that suit this region; and the frequenters of these paths go their natural gaits, in calf-skin or rubber boots, or bare-footed. The girdle of conventionality is laid aside, and the skirts rise with the spirits.

A stream that flows through a country of upland farms will show you many a pretty bit of genre painting. Here is the laundry-pool at the foot of the kitchen garden, and the tubs are set upon a few planks close to the water, and the farmer's daughters, with bare arms and gowns tucked up, are wringing out the clothes. Do you remember what happened to Ralph Peden in The Lilac Sunbonnet when he came on a scene like this? He tumbled at once into love with Winsome Charteris,--and far over his head.

And what a pleasant thing it is to see a little country lad riding one of the plough-horses to water, thumping his naked heels against the ribs of his stolid steed, and pulling hard on the halter as if it were the bridle of Bucephalus! Or perhaps it is a riotous company of boys that have come down to the old swimming-hole, and are now splashing and gambolling through the water like a drove of white seals very much sun-burned. You had hoped to catch a goodly trout in that hole, but what of that? The sight of a harmless hour of mirth is better than a fish, any day.

Possibly you will overtake another fisherman on the stream. It may be one of those fabulous countrymen, with long cedar poles and bed- cord lines, who are commonly reported to catch such enormous strings of fish, but who rarely, so far as my observation goes, do anything more than fill their pockets with fingerlings. The trained angler, who uses the finest tackle, and drops his fly on the water as accurately as Henry James places a word in a story, is the man who takes the most and the largest fish in the long run. Perhaps the fisherman ahead of you is such an one,--a man whom you have known in town as a lawyer or a doctor, a merchant or a preacher, going about his business in the hideous respectability of a high silk hat and a long black coat.

How good it is to see him now in the freedom of a flannel shirt and a broad-brimmed gray felt with flies stuck around the band.

In Professor John Wilson's Essays Critical and Imaginative, there is a brilliant description of a bishop fishing, which I am sure is drawn from the life: "Thus a bishop, sans wig and petticoat, in a hairy cap, black jacket, corduroy breeches and leathern leggins, creel on back and rod in hand, sallying from his palace, impatient to reach a famous salmon-cast ere the sun leave his cloud, . . . appears not only a pillar of his church, but of his kind, and in such a costume is manifestly on the high road to Canterbury and the Kingdom-Come." I have had the good luck to see quite a number of bishops, parochial and diocesan, in that style, and the vision has always dissolved my doubts in regard to the validity of their claim to the true apostolic succession.

Men's "little ways" are usually more interesting, and often more instructive than their grand manners. When they are off guard, they frequently show to better advantage than when they are on parade. I get more pleasure out of Boswell's Johnson than I do out of Rasselas or The Rambler. The Little Flowers of St. Francis appear to me far more precious than the most learned German and French analyses of his character. There is a passage in Jonathan Edwards' Personal Narrative, about a certain walk that he took in the fields near his father's house, and the blossoming of the flowers in the spring, which I would not exchange for the whole of his dissertation On the Freedom of the Will. And the very best thing of Charles Darwin's that I know is a bit from a letter to his wife: "At last I fell asleep," says he, "on the grass, and awoke with a chorus of birds singing around me, and squirrels running up the tree, and some woodpeckers laughing; and it was as pleasant and rural a scene as ever I saw; and I did not care one penny how any of the birds or beasts had been formed."

Little rivers have small responsibilities. They are not expected to bear huge navies on their breast or supply a hundred-thousand horse-power to the factories of a monstrous town. Neither do you come to them hoping to draw out Leviathan with a hook. It is enough if they run a harmless, amiable course, and keep the groves and fields green and fresh along their banks, and offer a happy alternation of nimble rapids and quiet pools,

"With here and there a lusty trout, And here and there a grayling."

When you set out to explore one of these minor streams in your canoe, you have no intention of epoch-making discoveries, or thrilling and world-famous adventures. You float placidly down the long stillwaters, and make your way patiently through the tangle of fallen trees that block the stream, and run the smaller falls, and carry your boat around the larger ones, with no loftier ambition than to reach a good camp-ground before dark and to pass the intervening hours pleasantly, "without offence to God or man." It is an agreeable and advantageous frame of mind for one who has done his fair share of work in the world, and is not inclined to grumble at his wages. There are few moods in which we are more susceptible of gentle instruction; and I suspect there are many tempers and attitudes, often called virtuous, in which the human spirit appears to less advantage in the sight of Heaven.

It is not required of every man and woman to be, or to do, something great; most of us must content ourselves with taking small parts in the chorus. Shall we have no little lyrics because Homer and Dante have written epics? And because we have heard the great organ at Freiburg, shall the sound of Kathi's zither in the alpine hut please us no more? Even those who have greatness thrust upon them will do well to lay the burden down now and then, and congratulate themselves that they are not altogether answerable for the conduct of the universe, or at least not all the time. "I reckon," said a cowboy to me one day, as we were riding through the Bad Lands of Dakota, "there's some one bigger than me, running this outfit. He can 'tend to it well enough, while I smoke my pipe after the round-up."

There is such a thing as taking ourselves and the world too seriously, or at any rate too anxiously. Half of the secular unrest and dismal, profane sadness of modern society comes from the vain idea that every man is bound to be a critic of life, and to let no day pass without finding some fault with the general order of things, or projecting some plan for its improvement. And the other half comes from the greedy notion that a man's life does consist, after all, in the abundance of the things that he possesses, and that it is somehow or other more respectable and pious to be always at work making a larger living, than it is to lie on your back in the green pastures and beside the still waters, and thank God that you are alive.

Come, then, my gentle reader, (for by this time you have discovered that this chapter is only a preface in disguise,--a declaration of principles or the want of them, an apology or a defence, as you choose to take it,) and if we are agreed, let us walk together; but if not, let us part here with out ill-will.

You shall not be deceived in this book. It is nothing but a handful of rustic variations on the old tune of "Rest and be thankful," a record of unconventional travel, a pilgrim's scrip with a few bits of blue-sky philosophy in it. There is, so far as I know, very little useful information and absolutely no criticism of the universe to be found in this volume. So if you are what Izaak Walton calls "a severe, sour-complexioned man," you would better carry it back to the bookseller, and get your money again, if he will give it to you, and go your way rejoicing after your own melancholy fashion.

But if you care for plain pleasures, and informal company, and friendly observations on men and things, (and a few true fish- stories,) then perhaps you may find something here not unworthy your perusal. And so I wish that your winter fire may burn clear and bright while you read these pages; and that the summer days may be fair, and the fish may rise merrily to your fly, whenever you follow one of these little rivers.

1895.

A LEAF OF SPEARMINT

RECOLLECTIONS OF A BOY AND A ROD.

"It puzzles me now, that I remember all these young impressions so, because I took no heed of them at the time whatever; and yet they come upon me bright, when nothing else is evident in the gray fog of experience."-- B. D. BLACKMORE: Lorna Doone.

Of all the faculties of the human mind, memory is the one that is most easily "led by the nose." There is a secret power in the sense of smell which draws the mind backward into the pleasant land of old times.

If you could paint a picture of Memory, in the symbolical manner of Quarles's Emblems, it should represent a man travelling the highway with a dusty pack upon his shoulders, and stooping to draw in a long, sweet breath from the small, deep-red, golden-hearted flowers of an old-fashioned rose-tree straggling through the fence of a neglected garden. Or perhaps, for a choice of emblems, you would better take a yet more homely and familiar scent: the cool fragrance of lilacs drifting through the June morning from the old bush that stands between the kitchen door and the well; the warm layer of pungent, aromatic air that floats over the tansy-bed in a still July noon; the drowsy dew of odour that falls from the big balm-of-Gilead tree by the roadside as you are driving homeward through the twilight of August; or, best of all, the clean, spicy, unexpected, unmistakable smell of a bed of spearmint--that is the bed whereon Memory loves to lie and dream!

Why not choose mint as the symbol of remembrance? It is the true spice-tree of our Northern clime, the myrrh and frankincense of the land of lingering snow. When its perfume rises, the shrines of the past are unveiled, and the magical rites of reminiscence begin.

I.

You are fishing down the Swiftwater in the early Spring. In a shallow pool, which the drought of summer will soon change into dry land, you see the pale-green shoots of a little plant thrusting themselves up between the pebbles, and just beginning to overtop the falling water. You pluck a leaf of it as you turn out of the stream to find a comfortable place for lunch, and, rolling it between your fingers to see whether it smells like a good salad for your bread and cheese, you discover suddenly that it is new mint. For the rest of that day you are bewitched; you follow a stream that runs through the country of Auld Lang Syne, and fill your creel with the recollections of a boy and a rod.

And yet, strangely enough, you cannot recall the boy himself at all distinctly. There is only the faintest image of him on the endless roll of films that has been wound through your mental camera: and in the very spots where his small figure should appear, it seems as if the pictures were always light-struck. Just a blur, and the dim outline of a new cap, or a well-beloved jacket with extra pockets, or a much-hated pair of copper-toed shoes--that is all you can see.

But the people that the boy saw, the companions who helped or hindered him in his adventures, the sublime and marvellous scenes among the Catskills and the Adirondacks and the Green Mountains, in the midst of which he lived and moved and had his summer holidays-- all these stand out sharp and clear, as the "Bab Ballads" say,

"Photographically lined On the tablets of your mind."

And most vivid do these scenes and people become when the vague and irrecoverable boy who walks among them carries a rod over his shoulder, and you detect the soft bulginess of wet fish about his clothing, and perhaps the tail of a big one emerging from his pocket. Then it seems almost as if these were things that had really happened, and of which you yourself were a great part.

The rod was a reward, yet not exactly of merit. It was an instrument of education in the hand of a father less indiscriminate than Solomon, who chose to interpret the text in a new way, and preferred to educate his child by encouraging him in pursuits which were harmless and wholesome, rather than by chastising him for practices which would likely enough never have been thought of, if they had not been forbidden. The boy enjoyed this kind of father at the time, and later he came to understand, with a grateful heart, that there is no richer inheritance in all the treasury of unearned blessings. For, after all, the love, the patience, the kindly wisdom of a grown man who can enter into the perplexities and turbulent impulses of a boy's heart, and give him cheerful companionship, and lead him on by free and joyful ways to know and choose the things that are pure and lovely and of good report, make as fair an image as we can find of that loving, patient Wisdom which must be above us all if any good is to come out of our childish race.

Now this was the way in which the boy came into possession of his undreaded rod. He was by nature and heredity one of those predestined anglers whom Izaak Walton tersely describes as "born so." His earliest passion was fishing. His favourite passage in Holy Writ was that place where Simon Peter throws a line into the sea and pulls out a great fish at the first cast.

But hitherto his passion had been indulged under difficulties--with improvised apparatus of cut poles, and flabby pieces of string, and bent pins, which always failed to hold the biggest fish; or perhaps with borrowed tackle, dangling a fat worm in vain before the noses of the staring, supercilious sunfish that poised themselves in the clear water around the Lake house dock at Lake George; or, at best, on picnic parties across the lake, marred by the humiliating presence of nurses, and disturbed by the obstinate refusal of old Horace, the boatman, to believe that the boy could bait his own hook, but sometimes crowned with the delight of bringing home a whole basketful of yellow perch and goggle-eyes. Of nobler sport with game fish, like the vaulting salmon and the merry, pugnacious trout, as yet the boy had only dreamed. But he had heard that there were such fish in the streams that flowed down from the mountains around Lake George, and he was at the happy age when he could believe anything--if it was sufficiently interesting.

There was one little river, and only one, within his knowledge and the reach of his short legs. It was a tiny, lively rivulet that came out of the woods about half a mile away from the hotel, and ran down cater-cornered through a sloping meadow, crossing the road under a flat bridge of boards, just beyond the root-beer shop at the lower end of the village. It seemed large enough to the boy, and he had long had his eye upon it as a fitting theatre for the beginning of a real angler's life. Those rapids, those falls, those deep, whirling pools with beautiful foam on them like soft, white custard, were they not such places as the trout loved to hide in?

You can see the long hotel piazza, with the gossipy groups of wooden chairs standing vacant in the early afternoon; for the grown-up people are dallying with the ultimate nuts and raisins of their mid-day dinner. A villainous clatter of innumerable little vegetable-dishes comes from the open windows of the pantry as the boy steals past the kitchen end of the house, with Horace's lightest bamboo pole over his shoulder, and a little brother in skirts and short white stockings tagging along behind him.

When they come to the five-rail fence where the brook runs out of the field, the question is, Over or under? The lowlier method seems safer for the little brother, as well as less conspicuous for persons who desire to avoid publicity until their enterprise has achieved success. So they crawl beneath a bend in the lowest rail,--only tearing one tiny three-cornered hole in a jacket, and making some juicy green stains on the white stockings,--and emerge with suppressed excitement in the field of the cloth of buttercups and daisies.

What an afternoon--how endless and yet how swift! What perilous efforts to leap across the foaming stream at its narrowest points; what escapes from quagmires and possible quicksands; what stealthy creeping through the grass to the edge of a likely pool, and cautious dropping of the line into an unseen depth, and patient waiting for a bite, until the restless little brother, prowling about below, discovers that the hook is not in the water at all, but lying on top of a dry stone,--thereby proving that patience is not the only virtue--or, at least, that it does a better business when it has a small vice of impatience in partnership with it!

How tired the adventurers grow as the day wears away; and as yet they have taken nothing! But their strength and courage return as if by magic when there comes a surprising twitch at the line in a shallow, unpromising rapid, and with a jerk of the pole a small, wiggling fish is whirled through the air and landed thirty feet back in the meadow.

"For pity's sake, don't lose him! There he is among the roots of the blue flag."

"I've got him! How cold he is--how slippery--how pretty! Just like a piece of rainbow!"

"Do you see the red spots? Did you notice how gamy he was, little brother; how he played? It is a trout, for sure; a real trout, almost as long as your hand."

So the two lads tramp along up the stream, chattering as if there were no rubric of silence in the angler's code. Presently another simple-minded troutling falls a victim to their unpremeditated art; and they begin already, being human, to wish for something larger. In the very last pool that they dare attempt--a dark hole under a steep bank, where the brook issues from the woods--the boy drags out the hoped-for prize, a splendid trout, longer than a new lead- pencil. But he feels sure that there must be another, even larger, in the same place. He swings his line out carefully over the water, and just as he is about to drop it in, the little brother, perched on the sloping brink, slips on the smooth pine-needles, and goes sliddering down into the pool up to his waist. How he weeps with dismay, and how funnily his dress sticks to him as he crawls out! But his grief is soon assuaged by the privilege of carrying the trout strung on an alder twig; and it is a happy, muddy, proud pair of urchins that climb over the fence out of the field of triumph at the close of the day.

What does the father say, as he meets them in the road? Is he frowning or smiling under that big brown beard? You cannot be quite sure. But one thing is clear: he is as much elated over the capture of the real trout as any one. He is ready to deal mildly with a little irregularity for the sake of encouraging pluck and perseverance. Before the three comrades have reached the hotel, the boy has promised faithfully never to take his little brother off again without asking leave; and the father has promised that the boy shall have a real jointed fishing-rod of his own, so that he will not need to borrow old Horace's pole any more.

At breakfast the next morning the family are to have a private dish; not an every-day affair of vulgar, bony fish that nurses can catch, but trout--three of them! But the boy looks up from the table and sees the adored of his soul, Annie V----, sitting at the other end of the room, and faring on the common food of mortals. Shall she eat the ordinary breakfast while he feasts on dainties? Do not other sportsmen send their spoils to the ladies whom they admire? The waiter must bring a hot plate, and take this largest trout to Miss V---- (Miss Annie, not her sister--make no mistake about it).

The face of Augustus is as solemn as an ebony idol while he plays his part of Cupid's messenger. The fair Annie affects surprise; she accepts the offering rather indifferently; her curls drop down over her cheeks to cover some small confusion. But for an instant the corner of her eye catches the boy's sidelong glance, and she nods perceptibly, whereupon his mother very inconsiderately calls attention to the fact that yesterday's escapade has sun-burned his face dreadfully.

Beautiful Annie V----, who, among all the unripened nymphs that played at hide-and-seek among the maples on the hotel lawn, or waded with white feet along the yellow beach beyond the point of pines, flying with merry shrieks into the woods when a boat-load of boys appeared suddenly around the corner, or danced the lancers in the big, bare parlours before the grown-up ball began--who in all that joyous, innocent bevy could be compared with you for charm or daring? How your dark eyes sparkled, and how the long brown ringlets tossed around your small head, when you stood up that evening, slim and straight, and taller by half a head than your companions, in the lamp-lit room where the children were playing forfeits, and said, "There is not one boy here that DARES to kiss ME!" Then you ran out on the dark porch, where the honeysuckle vines grew up the tall, inane Corinthian pillars.

Did you blame the boy for following? And were you very angry, indeed, about what happened,--until you broke out laughing at his cravat, which had slipped around behind his ear? That was the first time he ever noticed how much sweeter the honeysuckle smells at night than in the day. It was his entrance examination in the school of nature--human and otherwise. He felt that there was a whole continent of newly discovered poetry within him, and worshipped his Columbus disguised in curls. Your boy is your true idealist, after all, although (or perhaps because) he is still uncivilised.

II.

The arrival of the rod, in four joints, with an extra tip, a brass reel, and the other luxuries for which a true angler would willingly exchange the necessaries of life, marked a new epoch in the boy's career. At the uplifting of that wand, as if it had been in the hand of another Moses, the waters of infancy rolled back, and the way was opened into the promised land, whither the tyrant nurses, with all their proud array of baby-chariots, could not follow. The way was open, but not by any means dry. One of the first events in the dispensation of the rod was the purchase of a pair of high rubber boots. Inserted in this armour of modern infantry, and transfigured with delight, the boy clumped through all the little rivers within a circuit of ten miles from Caldwell, and began to learn by parental example the yet unmastered art of complete angling.

But because some of the streams were deep and strong, and his legs were short and slender, and his ambition was even taller than his boots, the father would sometimes take him up pickaback, and wade along carefully through the perilous places--which are often, in this world, the very places one longs to fish in. So, in your remembrance, you can see the little rubber boots sticking out under the father's arms, and the rod projecting over his head, and the bait dangling down unsteadily into the deep holes, and the delighted boy hooking and playing and basketing his trout high in the air. How many of our best catches in life are made from some one else's shoulders!

From this summer the whole earth became to the boy, as Tennyson describes the lotus country, "a land of streams." In school-days and in town he acknowledged the sway of those mysterious and irresistible forces which produce tops at one season, and marbles at another, and kites at another, and bind all boyish hearts to play mumble-the-peg at the due time more certainly than the stars are bound to their orbits. But when vacation came, with its annual exodus from the city, there was only one sign in the zodiac, and that was Pisces.

No country seemed to him tolerable without trout, and no landscape beautiful unless enlivened by a young river. Among what delectable mountains did those watery guides lead his vagrant steps, and with what curious, mixed, and sometimes profitable company did they make him familiar!

There was one exquisite stream among the Alleghanies, called Lycoming Creek, beside which the family spent a summer in a decadent inn, kept by a tremulous landlord who was always sitting on the steps of the porch, and whose most memorable remark was that he had "a misery in his stomach." This form of speech amused the boy, but he did not in the least comprehend it. It was the description of an unimaginable experience in a region which was as yet known to him only as the seat of pleasure. He did not understand how any one could be miserable when he could catch trout from his own dooryard.

The big creek, with its sharp turns from side to side of the valley, its hemlock-shaded falls in the gorge, and its long, still reaches in the "sugar-bottom," where the maple-trees grew as if in an orchard, and the superfluity of grasshoppers made the trout fat and dainty, was too wide to fit the boy. But nature keeps all sizes in her stock, and a smaller stream, called Rocky Run, came tumbling down opposite the inn, as if made to order for juvenile use.

How well you can follow it, through the old pasture overgrown with alders, and up past the broken-down mill-dam and the crumbling sluice, into the mountain-cleft from which it leaps laughing! The water, except just after a rain-storm, is as transparent as glass-- old-fashioned window-glass, I mean, in small panes, with just a tinge of green in it, like the air in a grove of young birches. Twelve feet down in the narrow chasm below the falls, where the water is full of tiny bubbles, like Apollinaris, you can see the trout poised, with their heads up-stream, motionless, but quivering a little, as if they were strung on wires.

The bed of the stream has been scooped out of the solid rock. Here and there banks of sand have been deposited, and accumulations of loose stone disguise the real nature of the channel. Great boulders have been rolled down the alleyway and left where they chanced to stick; the stream must get around them or under them as best it can. But there are other places where everything has been swept clean; nothing remains but the primitive strata, and the flowing water merrily tickles the bare ribs of mother earth. Whirling stones, in the spring floods, have cut well-holes in the rock, as round and even as if they had been made with a drill, and sometimes you can see the very stone that sunk the well lying at the bottom. There are long, straight, sloping troughs through which the water runs like a mill-race. There are huge basins into which the water rumbles over a ledge, as if some one were pouring it very steadily out of a pitcher, and from which it glides away without a ripple, flowing over a smooth pavement of rock which shelves down from the shallow foot to the deep head of the pool.

The boy wonders how far he dare wade out along that slippery floor. The water is within an inch of his boot-tops now. But the slope seems very even, and just beyond his reach a good fish is rising. Only one step more, and then, like the wicked man in the psalm, his feet begin to slide. Slowly, and standing bolt upright, with the rod held high above his head, as if it must on no account get wet, he glides forward up to his neck in the ice-cold bath, gasping with amazement. There have been other and more serious situations in life into which, unless I am mistaken, you have made an equally unwilling and embarrassed entrance, and in which you have been surprised to find yourself not only up to your neck, but over,--and you are a lucky man if you have had the presence of mind to stand still for a moment, before wading out, and make sure at least of the fish that tempted you into your predicament.

But Rocky Run, they say, exists no longer. It has been blasted by miners out of all resemblance to itself, and bewitched into a dingy water-power to turn wheels for the ugly giant, Trade. It is only in the valley of remembrance that its current still flows like liquid air; and only in that country that you can still see the famous men who came and went along the banks of the Lyocoming when the boy was there.

There was Collins, who was a wondrous adept at "daping, dapping, or dibbling" with a grasshopper, and who once brought in a string of trout which he laid out head to tail on the grass before the house in a line of beauty forty-seven feet long. A mighty bass voice had this Collins also, and could sing, "Larboard Watch, Ahoy!" "Down in a Coal-Mine," and other profound ditties in a way to make all the glasses on the table jingle; but withal, as you now suspect, rather a fishy character, and undeserving of the unqualified respect which the boy had for him. And there was Dr. Romsen, lean, satirical, kindly, a skilful though reluctant physician, who regarded it as a personal injury if any one in the party fell sick in summer time; and a passionately unsuccessful hunter, who would sit all night in the crotch of a tree beside an alleged deer-lick, and come home perfectly satisfied if he had heard a hedgehog grunt. It was he who called attention to the discrepancy between the boy's appetite and his size by saying loudly at a picnic, "I wouldn't grudge you what you eat, my boy, if I could only see that it did you any good,"--which remark was not forgiven until the doctor redeemed his reputation by pronouncing a serious medical opinion, before a council of mothers, to the effect that it did not really hurt a boy to get his feet wet. That was worthy of Galen in his most inspired moment. And there was hearty, genial Paul Merit, whose mere company was an education in good manners, and who could eat eight hard-boiled eggs for supper without ruffling his equanimity; and the tall, thin, grinning Major, whom an angry Irishwoman once described as "like a comb, all back and teeth;" and many more were the comrades of the boy's father, all of whom he admired, (and followed when they would let him,) but none so much as the father himself, because he was the wisest, kindest, and merriest of all that merry crew, now dispersed to the uttermost parts of the earth and beyond.

Other streams played a part in the education of that happy boy: the Kaaterskill, where there had been nothing but the ghosts of trout for the last thirty years, but where the absence of fish was almost forgotten in the joy of a first introduction to Dickens, one very showery day, when dear old Ned Mason built a smoky fire in a cave below Haines's Falls, and, pulling The Old Curiosity Shop out of his pocket, read aloud about Little Nell until the tears ran down the cheeks of reader and listener--the smoke was so thick, you know: and the Neversink, which flows through John Burroughs's country, and past one house in particular, perched on a high bluff, where a very dreadful old woman come out and throws stones at "city fellers fishin' through her land" (as if any one wanted to touch her land! It was the water that ran over it, you see, that carried the fish with it, and they were not hers at all): and the stream at Healing Springs, in the Virginia mountains, where the medicinal waters flow down into a lovely wild brook without injuring the health of the trout in the least, and where the only drawback to the angler's happiness is the abundance of rattlesnakes--but a boy does not mind such things as that; he feels as if he were immortal. Over all these streams memory skips lightly, and strikes a trail through the woods to the Adirondacks, where the boy made his first acquaintance with navigable rivers,--that is to say, rivers which are traversed by canoes and hunting-skiffs, but not yet defiled by steamboats,--and slept, or rather lay awake, for the first time on a bed of balsam-boughs in a tent.

III.

The promotion from all-day picnics to a two weeks' camping-trip is like going from school to college. By this time a natural process of evolution has raised the first rod to something lighter and more flexible,--a fly-rod, so to speak, but not a bigoted one,--just a serviceable, unprejudiced article, not above using any kind of bait that may be necessary to catch the fish. The father has received the new title of "governor," indicating not less, but more authority, and has called in new instructors to carry on the boy's education: real Adirondack guides--old Sam Dunning and one-eyed Enos, the last and laziest of the Saranac Indians. Better men will be discovered for later trips, but none more amusing, and none whose woodcraft seems more wonderful than that of this queerly matched team, as they make the first camp in a pelting rain-storm on the shore of Big Clear Pond. The pitching of the tents is a lesson in architecture, the building of the camp-fire a victory over damp nature, and the supper of potatoes and bacon and fried trout a veritable triumph of culinary art.

At midnight the rain is pattering persistently on the canvas; the fronts flaps are closed and tied together; the lingering fire shines through them, and sends vague shadows wavering up and down: the governor is rolled up in his blankets, sound asleep. It is a very long night for the boy.

What is that rustling noise outside the tent? Probably some small creature, a squirrel or a rabbit. Rabbit stew would be good for breakfast. But it sounds louder now, almost loud enough to be a fox,--there are no wolves left in the Adirondacks, or at least only a very few. That is certainly quite a heavy footstep prowling around the provision-box. Could it be a panther,--they step very softly for their size,--or a bear perhaps? Sam Dunning told about catching one in a trap just below here. (Ah, my boy, you will soon learn that there is no spot in all the forests created by a bountiful Providence so poor as to be without its bear story.) Where was the rifle put? There it is, at the foot of the tent- pole. Wonder if it is loaded?

"Waugh-ho! Waugh-ho-o-o-o!"

The boy springs from his blankets like a cat, and peeps out between the tent-flaps. There sits Enos, in the shelter of a leaning tree by the fire, with his head thrown back and a bottle poised at his mouth. His lonely eye is cocked up at a great horned owl on the branch above him. Again the sudden voice breaks out:

"Whoo! whoo! whoo cooks for you all?"

Enos puts the bottle down, with a grunt, and creeps off to his tent.

"De debbil in dat owl," he mutters. "How he know I cook for dis camp? How he know 'bout dat bottle? Ugh!"

There are hundreds of pictures that flash into light as the boy goes on his course, year after year, through the woods. There is the luxurious camp on Tupper's Lake, with its log cabins in the spruce-grove, and its regiment of hungry men who ate almost a deer a day; and there is the little bark shelter on the side of Mount Marcy, where the governor and the boy, with baskets full of trout from the Opalescent River, are spending the night, with nothing but a fire to keep them warm. There is the North Bay at Moosehead, with Joe La Croix (one more Frenchman who thinks he looks like Napoleon) posing on the rocks beside his canoe, and only reconciled by his vanity to the wasteful pastime of taking photographs while the big fish are rising gloriously out at the end of the point. There is the small spring-hole beside the Saranac River, where Pliny Robbins and the boy caught twenty-three noble trout, weighing from one to three pounds apiece, in the middle of a hot August afternoon, and hid themselves in the bushes when ever they heard a party coming down the river, because they did not care to attract company; and there are the Middle Falls, where the governor stood on a long spruce log, taking two-pound fish with the fly, and stepping out at every cast a little nearer to the end of the log, until it slowly tipped with him, and he settled down into the river.

Among such scenes as these the boy pursued his education, learning many things that are not taught in colleges; learning to take the weather as it comes, wet or dry, and fortune as it falls, good or bad; learning that a meal which is scanty fare for one becomes a banquet for two--provided the other is the right person; learning that there is some skill in everything, even in digging bait, and that what is called luck consists chiefly in having your tackle in good order; learning that a man can be just as happy in a log shanty as in a brownstone mansion, and that the very best pleasures are those that do not leave a bad taste in the mouth. And in all this the governor was his best teacher and his closest comrade.

Dear governor, you have gone out of the wilderness now, and your steps will be no more beside these remembered little rivers--no more, forever and forever. You will not come in sight around any bend of this clear Swiftwater stream where you made your last cast; your cheery voice will never again ring out through the deepening twilight where you are lingering for your disciple to catch up with you; he will never again hear you call: "Hallo, my boy! What luck? Time to go home!" But there is a river in the country where you have gone, is there not?--a river with trees growing all along it-- evergreen trees; and somewhere by those shady banks, within sound of clear running waters, I think you will be dreaming and waiting for your boy, if he follows the trail that you have shown him even to the end.

1895.

AMPERSAND

It is not the walking merely, it is keeping yourself in tune for a walk, in the spiritual and bodily condition in which you can find entertainment and exhilaration in so simple and natural a pastime. You are eligible to any good fortune when you are in a condition to enjoy a walk. When the air and water taste sweet to you, how much else will taste sweet! When the exercise of your limbs affords you pleasure, and the play of your senses upon the various objects and shows of Nature quickens and stimulates your spirit, your relation to the world and to yourself is what it should be,--simple, and direct, and wholesome."--JOHN BURROUGHS: Pepacton.

The right to the name of Ampersand, like the territory of Gaul in those Commentaries which Julius Caesar wrote for the punishment of schoolboys, is divided into three parts. It belongs to a mountain, and a lake, and a little river.

The mountain stands in the heart of the Adirondack country, just near enough to the thoroughfare of travel for thousands of people to see it every year, and just far enough from the beaten track to be unvisited except by a very few of the wise ones, who love to turn aside. Behind the mountain is the lake, which no lazy man has ever seen. Out of the lake flows the stream, winding down a long, untrodden forest valley, to join the Stony Creek waters and empty into the Raquette River.

Which of the three Ampersands has the prior claim to the name, I cannot tell. Philosophically speaking, the mountain ought to be regarded as the head of the family, because it was undoubtedly there before the others. And the lake was probably the next on the ground, because the stream is its child. But man is not strictly just in his nomenclature; and I conjecture that the little river, the last-born of the three, was the first to be christened Ampersand, and then gave its name to its parent and grand-parent. It is such a crooked stream, so bent and curved and twisted upon itself, so fond of turning around unexpected corners and sweeping away in great circles from its direct course, that its first explorers christened it after the eccentric supernumerary of the alphabet which appears in the old spelling-books as &--and per se, and.

But in spite of this apparent subordination to the stream in the matter of a name, the mountain clearly asserts its natural authority. It stands up boldly; and not only its own lake, but at least three others, the Lower Saranac, Round Lake, and Lonesome Pond, lie at its foot and acknowledge its lordship. When the cloud is on its brow, they are dark. When the sunlight strikes it, they smile.

Wherever you may go over the waters of these lakes you shall see Mount Ampersand looking down at you, and saying quietly, "This is my domain."

I never look at a mountain which asserts itself in this fashion without desiring to stand on the top of it. If one can reach the summit, one becomes a sharer in the dominion. The difficulties in the way only add to the zest of the victory. Every mountain is, rightly considered, an invitation to climb. And as I was resting for a month one summer at Bartlett's, Ampersand challenged me daily.

Did you know Bartlett's in its palmy time? It was the homeliest, quaintest, coziest place in the Adirondacks. Away back in the ante-bellum days Virgil Bartlett had come into the woods, and built his house on the bank of the Saranac River, between the Upper Saranac and Round Lake. It was then the only dwelling within a circle of many miles. The deer and bear were in the majority. At night one could sometimes hear the scream of the panther or the howling of wolves. But soon the wilderness began to wear the traces of a conventional smile. The desert blossomed a little--if not as the rose, at least as the gilly-flower. Fields were cleared, gardens planted; half a dozen log cabins were scattered along the river; and the old house, having grown slowly and somewhat irregularly for twenty years, came out, just before the time of which I write, in a modest coat of paint and a broad- brimmed piazza. But Virgil himself, the creator of the oasis--well known of hunters and fishermen, dreaded of lazy guides and quarrelsome lumbermen,--"Virge," the irascible, kind-hearted, indefatigable, was there no longer. He had made his last clearing, and fought his last fight; done his last favour to a friend, and thrown his last adversary out of the tavern door. His last log had gone down the river. His camp-fire had burned out. Peace to his ashes. His wife, who had often played the part of Abigail toward travellers who had unconsciously incurred the old man's mistrust, now reigned in his stead; and there was great abundance of maple- syrup on every man's flapjack.

The charm of Bartlett's for the angler was the stretch of rapid water in front of the house. The Saranac River, breaking from its first resting-place in the Upper Lake, plunged down through a great bed of rocks, making a chain of short falls and pools and rapids, about half a mile in length. Here, in the spring and early summer, the speckled trout--brightest and daintiest of all fish that swim-- used to be found in great numbers. As the season advanced, they moved away into the deep water of the lakes. But there were always a few stragglers left, and I have taken them in the rapids at the very end of August. What could be more delightful than to spend an hour or two, in the early morning or evening of a hot day, in wading this rushing stream, and casting the fly on its clear waters? The wind blows softly down the narrow valley, and the trees nod from the rocks above you. The noise of the falls makes constant music in your ears. The river hurries past you, and yet it is never gone.

The same foam-flakes seem to be always gliding downward, the same spray dashing over the stones, the same eddy coiling at the edge of the pool. Send your fly in under those cedar branches, where the water swirls around by that old log. Now draw it up toward the foam. There is a sudden gleam of dull gold in the white water. You strike too soon. Your line comes back to you. In a current like this, a fish will almost always hook himself. Try it again. This time he takes the fly fairly, and you have him. It is a good fish, and he makes the slender rod bend to the strain. He sulks for a moment as if uncertain what to do, and then with a rush darts into the swiftest part of the current. You can never stop him there. Let him go. Keep just enough pressure on him to hold the hook firm, and follow his troutship down the stream as if he were a salmon. He slides over a little fall, gleaming through the foam, and swings around in the next pool. Here you can manage him more easily; and after a few minutes' brilliant play, a few mad dashes for the current, he comes to the net, and your skilful guide lands him with a quick, steady sweep of the arm. The scales credit him with an even pound, and a better fish than this you will hardly take here in midsummer.

"On my word, master," says the appreciative Venator, in Walton's Angler, "this is a gallant trout; what shall we do with him?" And honest Piscator, replies: "Marry! e'en eat him to supper; we'll go to my hostess from whence we came; she told me, as I was going out of door, that my brother Peter, [and who is this but Romeyn of Keeseville?] a good angler and a cheerful companion, had sent word he would lodge there tonight, and bring a friend with him. My hostess has two beds, and I know you and I have the best; we'll rejoice with my brother Peter and his friend, tell tales, or sing ballads, or make a catch, or find some harmless sport to content us, and pass away a little time without offence to God or man."

Ampersand waited immovable while I passed many days in such innocent and healthful pleasures as these, until the right day came for the ascent. Cool, clean, and bright, the crystal morning promised a glorious noon, and the mountain almost seemed to beckon us to come up higher. The photographic camera and a trustworthy lunch were stowed away in the pack-basket. The backboard was adjusted at a comfortable angle in the stern seat of our little boat. The guide held the little craft steady while I stepped into my place; then he pushed out into the stream, and we went swiftly down toward Round Lake.

A Saranac boat is one of the finest things that the skill of man has ever produced under the inspiration of the wilderness. It is a frail shell, so light that a guide can carry it on his shoulders with ease, but so dexterously fashioned that it rides the heaviest waves like a duck, and slips through the water as if by magic. You can travel in it along the shallowest rivers and across the broadest lakes, and make forty or fifty miles a day, if you have a good guide.

Everything depends, in the Adirondacks, as in so many other regions of life, upon your guide. If he is selfish, or surly, or stupid, you will have a bad time. But if he is an Adirondacker of the best old-fashioned type,--now unhappily growing more rare from year to year,--you will find him an inimitable companion, honest, faithful, skilful and cheerful. He is as independent as a prince, and the gilded youths and finicking fine ladies who attempt to patronise him are apt to make but a sorry show before his solid and undisguised contempt. But deal with him man to man, and he will give you a friendly, loyal service which money cannot buy, and teach you secrets of woodcraft and lessons in plain, self-reliant manhood more valuable than all the learning of the schools. Such a guide was mine, rejoicing in the Scriptural name of Hosea, but commonly called, in brevity and friendliness, "Hose."

As we entered Round Lake on this fair morning, its surface was as smooth and shining as a mirror. It was too early yet for the tide of travel which sends a score of boats up and down this thoroughfare every day; and from shore to shore the water was unruffled, except by a flock of sheldrakes which had been feeding near Plymouth Rock, and now went skittering off into Weller Bay with a motion between flying and swimming, leaving a long wake of foam behind them.

At such a time as this you can see the real colour of these Adirondack lakes.

It is not blue, as romantic writers so often describe it, nor green, like some of those wonderful Swiss lakes; although of course it reflects the colour of the trees along the shore; and when the wind stirs it, it gives back the hue of the sky, blue when it is clear, gray when the clouds are gathering, and sometimes as black as ink under the shadow of storm. But when it is still, the water itself is like that river which one of the poets has described as

"Flowing with a smooth brown current."

And in this sheet of burnished bronze the mountains and islands were reflected perfectly, and the sun shone back from it, not in broken gleams or a wide lane of light, but like a single ball of fire, moving before us as we moved.

But stop! What is that dark speck on the water, away down toward Turtle Point? It has just the shape and size of a deer's head. It seems to move steadily out into the lake. There is a little ripple, like a wake, behind it. Hose turns to look at it, and then sends the boat darting in that direction with long, swift strokes. It is a moment of pleasant excitement, and we begin to conjecture whether the deer is a buck or a doe, and whose hounds have driven it in. But when Hose turns to look again, he slackens his stroke, and says: "I guess we needn't to hurry; he won't get away. It's astonishin' what a lot of fun a man can get in the course of a natural life a-chasm' chumps of wood."

We landed on a sand beach at the mouth of a little stream, where a blazed tree marked the beginning of the Ampersand trail. This line through the forest was made years ago by that ardent sportsman and lover of the Adirondacks, Dr. W. W. Ely, of Rochester. Since that time it has been shortened and improved a little by other travellers, and also not a little blocked and confused by the lumbermen and the course of Nature. For when the lumbermen go into the woods, they cut roads in every direction, leading nowhither, and the unwary wanderer is thereby led aside from the right way, and entangled in the undergrowth. And as for Nature, she is entirely opposed to continuance of paths through her forest. She covers them with fallen leaves, and hides them with thick bushes. She drops great trees across them, and blots then out with windfalls. But the blazed line--a succession of broad axe-marks on the trunks of the trees, just high enough to catch the eye on a level--cannot be so easily obliterated, and this, after all, is the safest guide through the woods.

Our trail led us at first through a natural meadow, overgrown with waist-high grass, and very spongy to the tread. Hornet-haunted also was this meadow, and therefore no place for idle dalliance or unwary digression, for the sting of the hornet is one of the saddest and most humiliating surprises of this mortal life.

Then through a tangle of old wood-roads my guide led me safely, and we struck one of the long ridges which slope gently from the lake to the base of the mountain. Here walking was comparatively easy, for in the hard-wood timber there is little underbrush. The massive trunks seemed like pillars set to uphold the level roof of green. Great yellow birches, shaggy with age, stretched their knotted arms high above us; sugar-maples stood up straight and proud under their leafy crowns; and smooth beeches--the most polished and parklike of all the forest trees--offered opportunities for the carving of lovers' names in a place where few lovers ever come.

The woods were quiet. It seemed as if all living creatures had deserted them. Indeed, if you have spent much time in our Northern forests, you must have often wondered at the sparseness of life, and felt a sense of pity for the apparent loneliness of the squirrel that chatters at you as you pass, or the little bird that hops noiselessly about in the thickets. The midsummer noontide is an especially silent time. The deer are asleep in some wild meadow. The partridge has gathered her brood for their midday nap. The squirrels are perhaps counting over their store of nuts in a hollow tree, and the hermit-thrush spares his voice until evening. The woods are close--not cool and fragrant as the foolish romances describe them--but warm and still; for the breeze which sweeps across the hilltop and ruffles the lake does not penetrate into these shady recesses, and therefore all the inhabitants take the noontide as their hour of rest. Only the big woodpecker--he of the scarlet head and mighty bill--is indefatigable, and somewhere unseen is "tapping the hollow beech-tree," while a wakeful little bird,--I guess it is the black-throated green warbler,--prolongs his dreamy, listless ditty,--'te-de-terit-sca,--'te-de-us--wait.

After about an hour of easy walking, our trail began to ascend more sharply. We passed over the shoulder of a ridge and around the edge of a fire-slash, and then we had the mountain fairly before us. Not that we could see anything of it, for the woods still shut us in, but the path became very steep, and we knew that it was a straight climb; not up and down and round about did this most uncompromising trail proceed, but right up, in a direct line for the summit.

Now this side of Ampersand is steeper than any Gothic roof I have ever seen, and withal very much encumbered with rocks and ledges and fallen trees. There were places where we had to haul ourselves up by roots and branches, and places where we had to go down on our hands and knees to crawl under logs. It was breathless work, but not at all dangerous or difficult. Every step forward was also a step upward; and as we stopped to rest for a moment, we could see already glimpses of the lake below us. But at these I did not much care to look, for I think it is a pity to spoil the surprise of a grand view by taking little snatches of it beforehand. It is better to keep one's face set to the mountain, and then, coming out from the dark forest upon the very summit, feel the splendour of the outlook flash upon one like a revelation.

The character of the woods through which we were now passing was entirely different from those of the lower levels. On these steep places the birch and maple will not grow, or at least they occur but sparsely. The higher slopes and sharp ridges of the mountains are always covered with soft-wood timber. Spruce and hemlock and balsam strike their roots among the rocks, and find a hidden nourishment. They stand close together; thickets of small trees spring up among the large ones; from year to year the great trunks are falling one across another, and the undergrowth is thickening around them, until a spruce forest seems to be almost impassable. The constant rain of needles and the crumbling of the fallen trees form a rich, brown mould, into which the foot sinks noiselessly. Wonderful beds of moss, many feet in thickness, and softer than feathers, cover the rocks and roots. There are shadows never broken by the sun, and dark, cool springs of icy water hidden away in the crevices. You feel a sense of antiquity here which you can never feel among the maples and birches. Longfellow was right when he filled his forest primeval with "murmuring pines and hemlocks."

The higher one climbs, the darker and gloomier and more rugged the vegetation becomes. The pine-trees soon cease to follow you; the hemlocks disappear, and the balsams can go no farther. Only the hardy spruce keeps on bravely, rough and stunted, with branches matted together and pressed down flat by the weight of the winter's snow, until finally, somewhere about the level of four thousand feet above the sea, even this bold climber gives out, and the weather-beaten rocks of the summit are clad only with mosses and Alpine plants.

Thus it is with mountains, as perhaps with men, a mark of superior dignity to be naturally bald.

Ampersand, falling short by a thousand feet of the needful height, cannot claim this distinction. But what Nature has denied, human labour has supplied. Under the direction of the Adirondack Survey, some years ago, several acres of trees were cut from the summit; and when we emerged, after the last sharp scramble, upon the very crest of the mountain, we were not shut in by a dense thicket, but stood upon a bare ridge of granite in the centre of a ragged clearing.

I shut my eyes for a moment, drew a few long breaths of the glorious breeze, and then looked out upon a wonder and a delight beyond description.

A soft, dazzling splendour filled the air. Snowy banks and drifts of cloud were floating slowly over a wide and wondrous land. Vast sweeps of forest, shining waters, mountains near and far, the deepest green and the palest blue, changing colours and glancing lights, and all so silent, so strange, so far away, that it seemed like the landscape of a dream. One almost feared to speak, lest it should vanish.

Right below us the Lower Saranac and Lonesome Pond, Round Lake and the Weller Ponds, were spread out like a map. Every point and island was clearly marked. We could follow the course of the Saranac River in all its curves and windings, and see the white tents of the hay-makers on the wild meadows. Far away to the northeast stretched the level fields of Bloomingdale. But westward all was unbroken wilderness, a great sea of woods as far as the eye could reach. And how far it can reach from a height like this! What a revelation of the power of sight! That faint blue outline far in the north was Lyon Mountain, nearly thirty miles away as the crow flies. Those silver gleams a little nearer were the waters of St. Regis. The Upper Saranac was displayed in all its length and breadth, and beyond it the innumerable waters of Fish

Creek were tangled among the dark woods. The long ranges of the hills about the Jordan bounded the western horizon, and on the southwest Big Tupper Lake was sleeping at the base of Mount Morris. Looking past the peak of Stony Creek Mountain, which rose sharp and distinct in a line with Ampersand, we could trace the path of the Raquette River from the distant waters of Long Lake down through its far- stretched valley, and catch here and there a silvery link of its current.

But when we turned to the south and east, how wonderful and how different was the view! Here was no widespread and smiling landscape with gleams of silver scattered through it, and soft blue haze resting upon its fading verge, but a wild land of mountains, stern, rugged, tumultuous, rising one beyond another like the waves of a stormy ocean,--Ossa piled upin Pelion,--Mcintyre's sharp peak, and the ragged crest of the Gothics, and, above all, Marcy's dome- like head, raised just far enough above the others to assert his royal right as monarch of the Adirondacks.

But grandest of all, as seen from this height, was Mount Seward,--a solemn giant of a mountain, standing apart from the others, and looking us full in the face. He was clothed from base to summit in a dark, unbroken robe of forest. Ou-kor-lah, the Indians called him--the Great Eye; and he seemed almost to frown upon us in defiance. At his feet, so straight below us that it seemed almost as if we could cast a stone into it, lay the wildest and most beautiful of all the Adirondack waters--Ampersand Lake.

On its shore, some five-and-twenty years ago, the now almost forgotten Adirondack Club had their shanty--the successor of "the Philosophers' Camp" on Follensbee Pond. Agassiz, Appleton, Norton, Emerson, Lowell, Hoar, Gray, John Holmes, and Stillman, were among the company who made their resting-place under the shadow of Mount Seward. They had bought a tract of forest land completely encircling the pond, cut a rough road to it through the woods, and built a comfortable log cabin, to which they purposed to return summer after summer. But the civil war broke out, with all its terrible excitement and confusion of hurrying hosts: the club existed but for two years, and the little house in the wilderness was abandoned. In 1878, when I spent three weeks at Ampersand, the cabin was in ruins, and surrounded by an almost impenetrable growth of bushes. The only philosophers to be seen were a family of what the guides quaintly call "quill pigs." The roof had fallen to the ground; raspberry-bushes thrust themselves through the yawning crevices between the logs; and in front of the sunken door-sill lay a rusty, broken iron stove, like a dismantled altar on which the fire had gone out forever.

After we had feasted upon the view as long as we dared, counted the lakes and streams, and found that we could see without a glass more than thirty, and recalled the memories of "good times" which came to us from almost every point of the compass, we unpacked the camera, and proceeded to take some pictures.

If you are a photographer, and have anything of the amateur's passion for your art, you will appreciate my pleasure and my anxiety. Never before, so far as I knew, had a camera been set up on Ampersand. I had but eight plates with me. The views were all very distant and all at a downward angle. The power of the light at this elevation was an unknown quantity. And the wind was sweeping vigorously across the open summit of the mountain. I put in my smallest stop, and prepared for short exposures.

My instrument was a thing called a Tourograph, which differs from most other cameras in having the plate-holder on top of the box. The plates are dropped into a groove below, and then moved into focus, after which the cap is removed and the exposure made.

I set my instrument for Ampersand Pond, sighted the picture through the ground glass, and measured the focus. Then I waited for a quiet moment, dropped the plate, moved it carefully forward to the proper mark, and went around to take off the cap. I found that I already had it in my hand, and the plate had been exposed for about thirty seconds with a sliding focus!

I expostulated with myself. I said: "You are excited; you are stupid; you are unworthy of the name of photographer. Light- writer! You ought to write with a whitewash-brush!" The reproof was effectual, and from that moment all went well. The plates dropped smoothly, the camera was steady, the exposure was correct. Six good pictures were made, to recall, so far as black and white could do it, the delights of that day.

It has been my good luck to climb many of the peaks of the Adirondacks--Dix, the Dial, Hurricane, the Giant of the Valley, Marcy, and Whiteface--but I do not think the outlook from any of them is so wonderful and lovely as that from little Ampersand: and I reckon among my most valuable chattels the plates of glass on which the sun has traced for me (who cannot draw) the outlines of that loveliest landscape.

The downward journey was swift. We halted for an hour or two beside a trickling spring, a few rods below the summit, to eat our lunch. Then, jumping, running, and sometimes sliding, we made the descent, passed in safety by the dreaded lair of the hornet, and reached Bartlett's as the fragrance of the evening pancake was softly diffused through the twilight. Mark that day, Memory, with a double star in your catalogue!

1895.

A HANDFUL OF HEATHER

"Scotland is the home of romance because it is the home of Scott, Burns, Black, Macdonald, Stevenson, and Barrie--and of thousands of men like that old Highlander in kilts on the tow-path, who loves what they have written. I would wager he has a copy of Burns in his sporran, and has quoted him half a dozen times to the grim Celt who is walking with him. Those old boys don't read for excitement or knowledge, but because they love their land and their people and their religion--and their great writers simply express their emotions for them in words they can understand. You and I come over here, with thousands of our countrymen, to borrow their emotions."--ROBERT BRIDGES: Overheard in Arcady.

My friend the Triumphant Democrat, fiercest of radicals and kindest of men, expresses his scorn for monarchical institutions (and his invincible love for his native Scotland) by tenanting, summer after summer, a famous castle among the heathery Highlands. There he proclaims the most uncompromising Americanism in a speech that grows more broadly Scotch with every week of his emancipation from the influence of the clipped, commercial accent of New York, and casts contempt on feudalism by playing the part of lord of the manor to such a perfection of high-handed beneficence that the people of the glen are all become his clansmen, and his gentle lady would be the patron saint of the district--if the republican theology of Scotland could only admit saints among the elect.

Every year he sends trophies of game to his friends across the sea-- birds that are as toothsome and wild-flavoured as if they had not been hatched under the tyranny of the game-laws. He has a pleasant trick of making them grateful to the imagination as well as to the palate by packing them in heather. I'll warrant that Aaron's rod bore no bonnier blossoms than these stiff little bushes--and none more magical. For every time I take up a handful of them they transport me to the Highlands, and send me tramping once more, with knapsack and fishing-rod, over the braes and down the burns.

I.

BELL-HEATHER.

Some of my happiest meanderings in Scotland have been taken under the lead of a book. Indeed, for travel in a strange country there can be no better courier. Not a guide-book, I mean, but a real book, and, by preference, a novel.

Fiction, like wine, tastes best in the place where it was grown. And the scenery of a foreign land (including architecture, which is artificial landscape) grows less dreamlike and unreal to our perception when we people it with familiar characters from our favourite novels. Even on a first journey we feel ourselves among old friends. Thus to read Romola in Florence, and Les Miserables in Paris, and Lorna Doone on Exmoor, and The Heart of Midlothian in Edinburgh, and David Balfour in the Pass of Glencoe, and The Pirate in the Shetland Isles, is to get a new sense of the possibilities of life. All these things have I done with much inward contentment; and other things of like quality have I yet in store; as, for example, the conjunction of The Bonnie Brier-Bush with Drumtochty, and The Little Minister with Thrums, and The Raiders with Galloway. But I never expect to pass pleasanter days than those I spent with A Princess of Thule among the Hebrides.

For then, to begin with, I was young; which is an unearned increment of delight sure to be confiscated by the envious years and never regained. But even youth itself was not to be compared with the exquisite felicity of being deeply and desperately in love with Sheila, the clear-eyed heroine of that charming book. In this innocent passion my gray-haired comrades, Howard Crosby, the Chancellor of the University of New York, and my father, an ex-Moderator of the Presbyterian General Assembly, were ardent but generous rivals.

How great is the joy and how fascinating the pursuit of such an ethereal affection! It enlarges the heart without embarrassing the conscience. It is a cup of pure gladness with no bitterness in its dregs. It spends the present moment with a free hand, and yet leaves no undesirable mortgage upon the future. King Arthur, the founder of the Round Table, expressed a conviction, according to Tennyson, that the most important element in a young knight's education is "the maiden passion for a maid." Surely the safest form in which this course in the curriculum may be taken is by falling in love with a girl in a book. It is the only affair of the kind into which a young fellow can enter without responsibility, and out of which he can always emerge, when necessary, without discredit. And as for the old fellow who still keeps up this education of the heart, and worships his heroine with the ardour of a John Ridd and the fidelity of a Henry Esmond, I maintain that he is exempt from all the penalties of declining years. The man who can love a girl in a book may be old, but never aged.

So we sailed, lovers all three, among the Western Isles, and whatever ship it was that carried us, her figurehead was always the Princess Sheila. Along the ruffled blue waters of the sounds and lochs that wind among the roots of unpronounceable mountains, and past the dark hills of Skye, and through the unnumbered flocks of craggy islets where the sea-birds nest, the spell of the sweet Highland maid drew us, and we were pilgrims to the Ultima Thule where she lived and reigned.

The Lewis, with its tail-piece, the Harris, is quite a sizable island to be appended to such a country as Scotland. It is a number of miles long, and another number of miles wide, and it has a number of thousand inhabitants--I should say as many as three- quarters of an inhabitant to the square mile--and the conditions of agriculture and the fisheries are extremely interesting and quarrelsome. All these I duly studied at the time, and reported in a series of intolerably dull letters to the newspaper which supplied a financial basis for my sentimental journey. They are full of information; but I have been amused to note, after these many years, how wide they steer of the true motive and interest of the excursion. There is not even a hint of Sheila in any of them. Youth, after all, is a shamefaced and secretive season; like the fringed polygala, it hides its real blossom underground.

It was Sheila's dark-blue dress and sailor hat with the white feather that we looked for as we loafed through the streets of Stornoway, that quaint metropolis of the herring-trade, where strings of fish alternated with boxes of flowers in the windows, and handfuls of fish were spread upon the roofs to dry just as the sliced apples are exposed upon the kitchen-sheds of New England in September, and dark-haired women were carrying great creels of fish on their shoulders, and groups of sunburned men were smoking among the fishing-boats on the beach and talking about fish, and sea- gulls were floating over the houses with their heads turning from side to side and their bright eyes peering everywhere for unconsidered trifles of fish, and the whole atmosphere of the place, physical, mental, and moral, was pervaded with fish. It was Sheila's soft, sing-song Highland speech that we heard through the long, luminous twilight in the pauses of that friendly chat on the balcony of the little inn where a good fortune brought us acquainted with Sam Bough, the mellow Edinburgh painter. It was Sheila's low sweet brow, and long black eyelashes, and tender blue eyes, that we saw before us as we loitered over the open moorland, a far-rolling sea of brown billows, reddened with patches of bell- heather, and brightened here and there with little lakes lying wide open to the sky. And were not these peat-cutters, with the big baskets on their backs, walking in silhouette along the ridges, the people that Sheila loved and tried to help; and were not these crofters' cottages with thatched roofs, like beehives, blending almost imperceptibly with the landscape, the dwellings into which she planned to introduce the luxury of windows; and were not these Standing Stones of Callernish, huge tombstones of a vanished religion, the roofless temple from which the Druids paid their westernmost adoration to the setting sun as he sank into the Atlantic--was not this the place where Sheila picked the bunch of wild flowers and gave it to her lover? There is nothing in history, I am sure, half so real to us as some of the things in fiction. The influence of an event upon our character is little affected by considerations as to whether or not it ever happened.

There were three churches in Stornoway, all Presbyterian, of course, and therefore full of pious emulation. The idea of securing an American preacher for an August Sabbath seemed to fall upon them simultaneously, and to offer the prospect of novelty without too much danger. The brethren of the U. P. congregation, being a trifle more gleg than the others, arrived first at the inn, and secured the promise of a morning sermon from Chancellor Howard Crosby. The session of the Free Kirk came in a body a little later, and to them my father pledged himself for the evening sermon. The senior elder of the Established Kirk, a snuff-taking man and very deliberate, was the last to appear, and to his request for an afternoon sermon there was nothing left to offer but the services of the young probationer in theology. I could see that it struck him as a perilous adventure. Questions about "the fundamentals" glinted in his watery eye. He crossed and uncrossed his legs with solemnity, and blew his nose so frequently in a huge red silk handkerchief that it seemed like a signal of danger. At last he unburdened himself of his hesitations.

"Ah'm not saying that the young man will not be orthodox--ahem! But ye know, sir, in the Kirk, we are not using hymns, but just the pure Psawms of Daffit, in the meetrical fairsion. And ye know, sir, they are ferry tifficult in the reating, whatefer, for a young man, and one that iss a stranger. And if his father will just be coming with him in the pulpit, to see that nothing iss said amiss, that will be ferry comforting to the congregation."

So the dear governor swallowed his laughter gravely and went surety for his son. They appeared together in the church, a barnlike edifice, with great galleries half-way between the floor and the roof. Still higher up, the pulpit stuck like a swallow's nest against the wall. The two ministers climbed the precipitous stair and found themselves in a box so narrow that one must stand perforce, while the other sat upon the only seat. In this "ride and tie" fashion they went through the service. When it was time to preach, the young man dropped the doctrines as discreetly as possible upon the upturned countenances beneath him. I have forgotten now what it was all about, but there was a quotation from the Song of Solomon, ending with "Sweet is thy voice, and thy countenance is comely." And when it came to that, the probationer's eyes (if the truth must be told) went searching through that sea of faces for one that should be familiar to his heart, and to which he might make a personal application of the Scripture passage--even the face of Sheila.

There are rivers in the Lewis, at least two of them, and on one of these we had the offer of a rod for a day's fishing. Accordingly we cast lots, and the lot fell upon the youngest, and I went forth with a tall, red-legged gillie, to try for my first salmon. The Whitewater came singing down out of the moorland into a rocky valley, and there was a merry curl of air on the pools, and the silver fish were leaping from the stream. The gillie handled the big rod as if it had been a fairy's wand, but to me it was like a giant's spear. It was a very different affair from fishing with five ounces of split bamboo on a Long Island trout-pond. The monstrous fly, like an awkward bird, went fluttering everywhere but in the right direction. It was the mercy of Providence that preserved the gillie's life. But he was very patient and forbearing, leading me on from one pool to another, as I spoiled the water and snatched the hook out of the mouth of rising fish, until at last we found a salmon that knew even less about the niceties of salmon-fishing than I did. He seized the fly firmly, before I could pull it away, and then, in a moment, I found myself attached to a creature with the strength of a whale and the agility of a flying-fish. He led me rushing up and down the bank like a madman. He played on the surface like a whirlwind, and sulked at the bottom like a stone. He meditated, with ominous delay, in the middle of the deepest pool, and then, darting across the river, flung himself clean out of water and landed far up on the green turf of the opposite shore. My heart melted like a snowflake in the sea, and I thought that I had lost him forever. But he rolled quietly back into the water with the hook still set in his nose. A few minutes afterwards I brought him within reach of the gaff, and my first salmon was glittering on the grass beside me.

Then I remembered that William Black had described this very fish in A Princess of Thule. I pulled the book from my pocket, and, lighting a pipe, sat down to read that delightful chapter over again. The breeze played softly down the valley. The warm sunlight was filled with the musical hum of insects and the murmur of falling waters. I thought how much pleasanter it would have been to learn salmon-fishing, as Black's hero did, from the Maid of Borva, than from a red-headed gillie. But, then, his salmon, after leaping across the stream, got away; whereas mine was safe. A man cannot have everything in this world. I picked a spray of rosy bell-heather from the bank of the river, and pressed it between the leaves of the book in memory of Sheila.

II.

COMMON HEATHER.

It is not half as far from Albany to Aberdeen as it is from New York to London. In fact, I venture to say that an American on foot will find himself less a foreigner in Scotland than in any other country in the Old World. There is something warm and hospitable-- if he knew the language well enough he would call it couthy--in the greeting that he gets from the shepherd on the moor, and the conversation that he holds with the farmer's wife in the stone cottage, where he stops to ask for a drink of milk and a bit of oat-cake. He feels that there must be a drop of Scotch somewhere in his mingled blood, or at least that the texture of his thought and feelings has been partly woven on a Scottish loom--perhaps the Shorter Catechism, or Robert Burns's poems, or the romances of Sir Walter Scott. At all events, he is among a kindred and comprehending people. They do not speak English in the same way that he does--through the nose---but they think very much more in his mental dialect than the English do. They are independent and wide awake, curious and full of personal interest. The wayside mind in Inverness or Perth runs more to muscle and less to fat, has more active vanity and less passive pride, is more inquisitive and excitable and sympathetic--in short, to use a symbolist's description, it is more apt to be red-headed--than in Surrey or Somerset. Scotchmen ask more questions about America, but fewer foolish ones. You will never hear them inquiring whether there is any good bear-hunting in the neighbourhood of Boston, or whether Shakespeare is much read in the States. They have a healthy respect for our institutions, and have quite forgiven (if, indeed, they ever resented) that little affair in 1776. They are all born Liberals. When a Scotchman says he is a Conservative, it only means that he is a Liberal with hesitations.

And yet in North Britain the American pedestrian will not find that amused and somewhat condescending toleration for his peculiarities, that placid willingness to make the best of all his vagaries of speech and conduct, that he finds in South Britain. In an English town you may do pretty much what you like on a Sunday, even to the extent of wearing a billycock hat to church, and people will put up with it from a countryman of Buffalo Bill and the Wild West Show. But in a Scotch village, if you whistle in the street on a Lord's Day, though it be a Moody and Sankey tune, you will be likely to get, as I did, an admonition from some long-legged, grizzled elder:

"Young man, do ye no ken it's the Sawbath Day?"

I recognised the reproof of the righteous, an excellent oil which doth not break the head, and took it gratefully at the old man's hands. For did it not prove that he regarded me as a man and a brother, a creature capable of being civilised and saved?

It was in the gray town of Dingwall that I had this bit of pleasant correction, as I was on the way to a fishing tramp through Sutherlandshire. This northwest corner of Great Britain is the best place in the whole island for a modest and impecunious angler. There are, or there were a few years ago, wild lochs and streams which are still practically free, and a man who is content with small things can pick up some very pretty sport from the highland inns, and make a good basket of memorable experiences every week.

The inn at Lairg, overlooking the narrow waters of Loch Shin, was embowered in honeysuckles, and full of creature comfort. But there were too many other men with rods there to suit my taste. "The feesh in this loch," said the boatman, "iss not so numerous ass the feeshermen, but more wise. There iss not one of them that hass not felt the hook, and they know ferry well what side of the fly has the forkit tail."

At Altnaharra, in the shadow of Ben Clebrig, there was a cozy little house with good fare, and abundant trout-fishing in Loch Naver and Loch Meadie. It was there that I fell in with a wandering pearl-peddler who gathered his wares from the mussels in the moorland streams. They were not of the finest quality, these Scotch pearls, but they had pretty, changeable colours of pink and blue upon them, like the iridescent light that plays over the heather in the long northern evenings. I thought it must be a hard life for the man, wading day after day in the ice-cold water, and groping among the coggly, sliddery stones for the shellfish, and cracking open perhaps a thousand before he could find one pearl. "Oh, yess," said be, "and it iss not an easy life, and I am not saying that it will be so warm and dry ass liffing in a rich house. But it iss the life that I am fit for, and I hef my own time and my thoughts to mysel', and that is a ferry goot thing; and then, sir, I haf found the Pearl of Great Price, and I think upon that day and night."

Under the black, shattered peaks of Ben Laoghal, where I saw an eagle poising day after day as if some invisible centripetal force bound him forever to that small circle of air, there was a loch with plenty of brown trout and a few salmo ferox; and down at Tongue there was a little river where the sea-trout sometimes come up with the tide.

Here I found myself upon the north coast, and took the road eastward between the mountains and the sea. It was a beautiful region of desolation. There were rocky glens cutting across the road, and occasionally a brawling stream ran down to the salt water, breaking the line of cliffs with a little bay and a half- moon of yellow sand. The heather covered all the hills. There were no trees, and but few houses. The chief signs of human labour were the rounded piles of peat, and the square cuttings in the moor marking the places where the subterranean wood-choppers had gathered their harvests. The long straths were once cultivated, and every patch of arable land had its group of cottages full of children. The human harvest has always been the richest and most abundant that is raised in the Highlands; but unfortunately the supply exceeded the demand; and so the crofters were evicted, and great flocks of sheep were put in possession of the land; and now the sheep-pastures have been changed into deer-forests; and far and wide along the valleys and across the hills there is not a trace of habitation, except the heaps of stones and the clumps of straggling bushes which mark the sites of lost homes. But what is one country's loss is another country's gain. Canada and the United States are infinitely the richer for the tough, strong, fearless, honest men that were dispersed from these lonely straths to make new homes across the sea.

It was after sundown when I reached the straggling village of Melvich, and the long day's journey had left me weary. But the inn, with its red-curtained windows, looked bright and reassuring. Thoughts of dinner and a good bed comforted my spirit--prematurely. For the inn was full. There were but five bedrooms and two parlours. The gentlemen who had the neighbouring shootings occupied three bedrooms and a parlour; the other two bedrooms had just been taken by the English fishermen who had passed me in the road an hour ago in the mail-coach (oh! why had I not suspected that treacherous vehicle?); and the landlord and his wife assured me, with equal firmness and sympathy, that there was not another cot or pair of blankets in the house. I believed them, and was sinking into despair when Sandy M'Kaye appeared on the scene as my angel of deliverance. Sandy was a small, withered, wiry man, dressed in rusty gray, with an immense white collar thrusting out its points on either side of his chin, and a black stock climbing over the top of it. I guessed from his speech that he had once lived in the lowlands. He had hoped to be engaged as a gillie by the shooting party, but had been disappointed. He had wanted to be taken by the English fishermen, but another and younger man had stepped in before him. Now Sandy saw in me his Predestinated Opportunity, and had no idea of letting it post up the road that night to the next village. He cleared his throat respectfully and cut into the conversation.

"Ah'm thinkin' the gentleman micht find a coomfortaible lodgin' wi' the weedow Macphairson a wee bittie doon the road. Her dochter is awa' in Ameriky, an' the room is a verra fine room, an' it is a peety to hae it stannin' idle, an' ye wudna mind the few steps to and fro tae yir meals here, sir, wud ye? An' if ye 'ill gang wi' me efter dinner, 'a 'll be prood to shoo ye the hoose."

So, after a good dinner with the English fishermen, Sandy piloted me down the road through the thickening dusk. I remember a hoodie crow flew close behind us with a choking, ghostly cough that startled me. The Macpherson cottage was a snug little house of stone, with fuchsias and roses growing in the front yard: and the widow was a douce old lady, with a face like a winter apple in the month of April, wrinkled, but still rosy. She was a little doubtful about entertaining strangers, but when she heard I was from America she opened the doors of her house and her heart. And when, by a subtle cross examination that would have been a credit to the wife of a Connecticut deacon, she discovered the fact that her lodger was a minister, she did two things, with equal and immediate fervour; she brought out the big Bible and asked him to conduct evening worship, and she produced a bottle of old Glenlivet and begged him to "guard against takkin' cauld by takkin' a glass of speerits."

It was a very pleasant fortnight at Melvich. Mistress Macpherson was so motherly that "takkin' cauld" was reduced to a permanent impossibility. The other men at the inn proved to be very companionable fellows, quite different from the monsters of insolence that my anger had imagined in the moment of disappointment. The shooting party kept the table abundantly supplied with grouse and hares and highland venison; and there was a piper to march up and down before the window and play while we ate dinner--a very complimentary and disquieting performance. But there are many occasions in life when pride can be entertained only at the expense of comfort.

Of course Sandy was my gillie. It was a fine sight to see him exhibiting the tiny American trout-rod, tied with silk ribbons in its delicate case, to the other gillies and exulting over them. Every morning he would lead me away through the heather to some lonely loch on the shoulders of the hills, from which we could look down upon the Northern Sea and the blue Orkney Isles far away across the Pentland Firth. Sometimes we would find a loch with a boat on it, and drift up and down, casting along the shores. Sometimes, in spite of Sandy's confident predictions, no boat could be found, and then I must put on the Mackintosh trousers and wade out over my hips into the water, and circumambulate the pond, throwing the flies as far as possible toward the middle, and feeling my way carefully along the bottom with the long net-handle, while Sandy danced on the bank in an agony of apprehension lest his Predestinated Opportunity should step into a deep hole and be drowned. It was a curious fact in natural history that on the lochs with boats the trout were in the shallow water, but in the boatless lochs they were away out in the depths. "Juist the total depraivity o' troots," said Sandy, "an' terrible fateegin'."

Sandy had an aversion to commit himself to definite statements on any subject not theological. If you asked him how long the morning's tramp would be, it was "no verra long, juist a bit ayant the hull yonner." And if, at the end of the seventh mile, you complained that it was much too far, he would never do more than admit that "it micht be shorter." If you called him to rejoice over a trout that weighed close upon two pounds, he allowed that it was "no bad--but there's bigger anes i' the loch gin we cud but wile them oot." And at lunch-time, when we turned out a full basket of shining fish on the heather, the most that he would say, while his eyes snapped with joy and pride, was, "Aweel, we canna complain, the day."

Then he would gather an armful of dried heather-stems for kindling, and dig out a few roots and crooked limbs of the long-vanished forest from the dry, brown, peaty soil, and make our campfire of prehistoric wood--just for the pleasant, homelike look of the blaze--and sit down beside it to eat our lunch. Heat is the least of the benefits that man gets from fire. It is the sign of cheerfulness and good comradeship. I would not willingly satisfy my hunger, even in a summer nooning, without a little flame burning on a rustic altar to consecrate and enliven the feast. When the bread and cheese were finished and the pipes were filled with Virginia tobacco, Sandy would begin to tell me, very solemnly and respectfully, about the mistakes I had made in the fishing that day, and mourn over the fact that the largest fish had not been hooked. There was a strong strain of pessimism in Sandy, and he enjoyed this part of the sport immensely.

But he was at his best in the walk home through the lingering twilight, when the murmur of the sea trembled through the air, and the incense of burning peat floated up from the cottages, and the stars blossomed one by one in the pale-green sky. Then Sandy dandered on at his ease down the hills, and discoursed of things in heaven and earth. He was an unconscious follower of the theology of the Reverend John Jasper, of Richmond, Virginia, and rejected the Copernican theory of the universe as inconsistent with the history of Joshua. "Gin the sun doesna muve," said he, "what for wad Joshua be tellin' him to stond steel? 'A wad suner beleeve there was a mistak' in the veesible heevens than ae fault in the Guid Buik." Whereupon we held long discourse of astronomy and inspiration; but Sandy concluded it with a philosophic word which left little to be said: "Aweel, yon teelescope is a wonnerful deescovery; but 'a dinna think the less o' the Baible."

III.

WHITE HEATHER.

Memory is a capricious and arbitrary creature. You never can tell what pebble she will pick up from the shore of life to keep among her treasures, or what inconspicuous flower of the field she will preserve as the symbol of

"Thoughts that do often lie too deep for tears."

She has her own scale of values for these mementos, and knows nothing of the market price of precious stones or the costly splendour of rare orchids. The thing that pleases her is the thing that she will hold fast. And yet I do not doubt that the most important things are always the best remembered; only we must learn that the real importance of what we see and hear in the world is to be measured at last by its meaning, its significance, its intimacy with the heart of our heart and the life of our life. And when we find a little token of the past very safely and imperishably kept among our recollections, we must believe that memory has made no mistake. It is because that little thing has entered into our experience most deeply, that it stays with us and we cannot lose it.

You have half forgotten many a famous scene that you travelled far to look upon. You cannot clearly recall the sublime peak of Mont Blanc, the roaring curve of Niagara, the vast dome of St. Peter's. The music of Patti's crystalline voice has left no distinct echo in your remembrance, and the blossoming of the century-plant is dimmer than the shadow of a dream. But there is a nameless valley among the hills where you can still trace every curve of the stream, and see the foam-bells floating on the pool below the bridge, and the long moss wavering in the current. There is a rustic song of a girl passing through the fields at sunset, that still repeats its far-off cadence in your listening ears. There is a small flower trembling on its stem in some hidden nook beneath the open sky, that never withers through all the changing years; the wind passes over it, but it is not gone--it abides forever in your soul, an amaranthine blossom of beauty and truth.

White heather is not an easy flower to find. You may look for it among the highlands for a day without success. And when it is discovered, there is little outward charm to commend it. It lacks the grace of the dainty bells that hang so abundantly from the Erica Tetralix, and the pink glow of the innumerable blossoms of the common heather. But then it is a symbol. It is the Scotch Edelweiss. It means sincere affection, and unselfish love, and tender wishes as pure as prayers. I shall always remember the evening when I found the white heather on the moorland above Glen Ericht. Or, rather, it was not I that found it (for I have little luck in the discovery of good omens, and have never plucked a four- leaved clover in my life), but my companion, the gentle Mistress of the Glen, whose hair was as white as the tiny blossoms, and yet whose eyes were far quicker than mine to see and name every flower that bloomed in those lofty, widespread fields.

Ericht Water is formed by the marriage of two streams, one flowing out of Strath Ardle and the other descending from Cairn Gowar through the long, lonely Pass of Glenshee. The Ericht begins at the bridge of Cally, and its placid, beautiful glen, unmarred by railway or factory, reaches almost down to

Blairgowrie. On the southern bank, but far above the water, runs the high road to Braemar and the Linn of Dee. On the other side of the river, nestling among the trees, is the low white manor-house,

"An ancient home of peace."

It is a place where one who had been wearied and perchance sore wounded in the battle of life might well desire to be carried, as Arthur to the island valley of Avilion, for rest and healing.

I have no thought of renewing the conflicts and cares that filled that summer with sorrow. There were fightings without and fears within; there was the surrender of an enterprise that had been cherished since boyhood, and the bitter sense of irremediable weakness that follows such a reverse; there was a touch of that wrath with those we love, which, as Coleridge says,

"Doth work like madness in the brain;"

flying across the sea from these troubles, I had found my old comrade of merrier days sentenced to death, and caught but a brief glimpse of his pale, brave face as he went away into exile. At such a time the sun and the light and the moon and the stars are darkened, and the clouds return after rain. But through those clouds the Mistress of the Glen came to meet me--a stranger till then, but an appointed friend, a minister of needed grace, an angel of quiet comfort. The thick mists of rebellion, mistrust, and despair have long since rolled away, and against the background of the hills her figure stands out clearly, dressed in the fashion of fifty years ago, with the snowy hair gathered close beneath her widow's cap, and a spray of white heather in her outstretched hand.

There were no other guests in the house by the river during those still days in the noontide hush of midsummer. Every morning, while the Mistress was busied with her household cares and letters, I would be out in the fields hearing the lark sing, and watching the rabbits as they ran to and fro, scattering the dew from the grass in a glittering spray. Or perhaps I would be angling down the river, with the swift pressure of the water around my knees, and an inarticulate current of cooling thoughts flowing on and on through my brain like the murmur of the stream. Every afternoon there were long walks with the Mistress in the old-fashioned garden, where wonderful roses were blooming; or through the dark, fir-shaded den where the wild burn dropped down to join the river; or out upon the high moor under the waning orange sunset. Every night there were luminous and restful talks beside the open fire in the library, when the words came clear and calm from the heart, unperturbed by the vain desire of saying brilliant things, which turns so much of our conversation into a combat of wits instead of an interchange of thoughts. Talk like this is possible only between two. The arrival of a third person sets the lists for a tournament, and offers the prize for a verbal victory. But where there are only two, the armour is laid aside, and there is no call to thrust and parry.

One of the two should be a good listener, sympathetic, but not silent, giving confidence in order to attract it--and of this art a woman is the best master. But its finest secrets do not come to her until she has passed beyond the uncertain season of compliments and conquests, and entered into the serenity of a tranquil age.

What is this foolish thing that men say about the impossibility of true intimacy and converse between the young and the old? Hamerton, for example, in his book on Human Intercourse, would have us believe that a difference in years is a barrier between hearts. For my part, I have more often found it an open door, and a security of generous and tolerant welcome for the young soldier, who comes in tired and dusty from the battle-field, to tell his story of defeat or victory in the garden of still thoughts where old age is resting in the peace of honourable discharge. I like what Robert Louis Stevenson says about it in his essay on Talk and Talkers.

"Not only is the presence of the aged in itself remedial, but their minds are stored with antidotes, wisdom's simples, plain considerations overlooked by youth. They have matter to communicate, be they never so stupid. Their talk is not merely literature, it is great literature; classic by virtue of the speaker's detachment; studded, like a book of travel, with things we should not otherwise have learnt. . . where youth agrees with age, not where they differ, wisdom lies; and it is when the young disciple finds his heart to beat in tune with his gray-haired teacher's that a lesson may be learned."

The conversation of the Mistress of the Glen shone like the light and distilled like the dew, not only by virtue of what she said, but still more by virtue of what she was. Her face was a good counsel against discouragement; and the cheerful quietude of her demeanour was a rebuke to all rebellious, cowardly, and discontented thoughts. It was not the striking novelty or profundity of her commentary on life that made it memorable, it was simply the truth of what she said and the gentleness with which she said it. Epigrams are worth little for guidance to the perplexed, and less for comfort to the wounded. But the plain, homely sayings which come from a soul that has learned the lesson of patient courage in the school of real experience, fall upon the wound like drops of balsam, and like a soothing lotion up on the eyes smarting and blinded with passion.

She spoke of those who had walked with her long ago in her garden, and for whose sake, now that they had all gone into the world of light, every flower was doubly dear. Would it be a true proof of loyalty to them if she lived gloomily or despondently because they were away? She spoke of the duty of being ready to welcome happiness as well as to endure pain, and of the strength that endurance wins by being grateful for small daily joys, like the evening light, and the smell of roses, and the singing of birds. She spoke of the faith that rests on the Unseen Wisdom and Love like a child on its mother's breast, and of the melting away of doubts in the warmth of an effort to do some good in the world. And if that effort has conflict, and adventure, and confused noise, and mistakes, and even defeats mingled with it, in the stormy years of youth, is not that to be expected? The burn roars and leaps in the den; the stream chafes and frets through the rapids of the glen; the river does not grow calm and smooth until it nears the sea. Courage is a virtue that the young cannot spare; to lose it is to grow old before the time; it is better to make a thousand mistakes and suffer a thousand reverses than to refuse the battle. Resignation is the final courage of old age; it arrives in its own season; and it is a good day when it comes to us. Then there are no more disappointments; for we have learned that it is even better to desire the things that we have than to have the things that we desire. And is not the best of all our hopes--the hope of immortality--always before us? How can we be dull or heavy while we have that new experience to look forward to? It will be the most joyful of all our travels and adventures. It will bring us our best acquaintances and friendships. But there is only one way to get ready for immortality, and that is to love this life, and live it as bravely and cheerfully and faithfully as we can.

So my gentle teacher with the silver hair showed me the treasures of her ancient, simple faith; and I felt that no sermons, nor books, nor arguments can strengthen the doubting heart so deeply as just to come into touch with a soul which has proved the truth of that plain religion whose highest philosophy is "Trust in the Lord and do good." At the end of the evening the household was gathered for prayers, and the Mistress kneeled among her servants, leading them, in her soft Scottish accent, through the old familiar petitions for pardon for the errors of the day, and refreshing sleep through the night and strength for the morrow. It is good to be in a land where the people are not ashamed to pray. I have shared the blessing of Catholics at their table in lowly huts among the mountains of the Tyrol, and knelt with Covenanters at their household altar in the glens of Scotland; and all around the world, where the spirit of prayer is, there is peace. The genius of the Scotch has made many contributions to literature, but none I think, more precious, and none that comes closer to the heart, than the prayer which Robert Louis Stevenson wrote for his family in distant Samoa, the night before he died:--

"We beseech thee, Lord, to behold us with favour, folk of many families and nations, gathered together in the peace of this roof: weak men and women subsisting under the covert of thy patience. Be patient still; suffer us yet a while longer--with our broken promises of good, with our idle endeavours against evil--suffer us a while longer to endure, and (if it may be) help us to do better. Bless to us our extraordinary mercies; if the day come when these must be taken, have us play the man under affliction. Be with our friends, be with ourselves. Go with each of us to rest; if any awake, temper to them the dark hours of watching; and when the day returns to us--our sun and comforter--call us with morning faces, eager to labour, eager to be happy, if happiness shall be our portion, and, if the day be marked to sorrow, strong to endure it. We thank thee and praise thee; and, in the words of Him to whom this day is sacred, close our oblation."

The man who made that kindly human prayer knew the meaning of white heather. And I dare to hope that I too have known something of its meaning, since that evening when the Mistress of the Glen picked the spray and gave it to me on the lonely moor. "And now," she said, "you will be going home across the sea; and you have been welcome here, but it is time that you should go, for there is the place where your real duties and troubles and joys are waiting for you. And if you have left any misunderstandings behind you, you will try to clear them up; and if there have been any quarrels, you will heal them. Carry this little flower with you. It's not the bonniest blossom in Scotland, but it's the dearest, for the message that it brings. And you will remember that love is not getting, but giving; not a wild dream of pleasure, and a madness of desire--oh no, love is not that--it is goodness, and honour, and peace, and pure living--yes, love is that; and it is the best thing in the world, and the thing that lives longest. And that is what I am wishing for you and yours with this bit of white heather."

1893.

THE RISTIGOUCHE FROM A HORSE-YACHT

Dr. Paley was ardently attached to this amusement; so much so that when the Bishop of Durham inquired of him when one of his most important works would be finished, he said, with great simplicity and good humour, 'My Lord, I shall work steadily at it when the fly-fishing season is over.'--SIR HUMPHRY DAVY: Salmonia.

The boundary line between the Province of Quebec and New Brunswick, for a considerable part of its course, resembles the name of the poet Keats; it is "writ in water." But like his fame, it is water that never fails,--the limpid current of the river Ristigouche.

The railway crawls over it on a long bridge at Metapedia, and you are dropped in the darkness somewhere between midnight and dawn. When you open your window-shutters the next morning, you see that the village is a disconsolate hamlet, scattered along the track as if it had been shaken by chance from an open freight-car; it consists of twenty houses, three shops, and a discouraged church perched upon a little hillock like a solitary mourner on the anxious seat. The one comfortable and prosperous feature in the countenance of Metapedia is the house of the Ristigouche Salmon Club--an old-fashioned mansion, with broad, white piazza, looking over rich meadowlands. Here it was that I found my friend Favonius, president of solemn societies, pillar of church and state, ingenuously arrayed in gray knickerbockers, a flannel shirt, and a soft hat, waiting to take me on his horse-yacht for a voyage up the river.

Have you ever seen a horse-yacht? Sometimes it is called a scow; but that sounds common. Sometimes it is called a house-boat; but that is too English. What does it profit a man to have a whole dictionary full of language at his service, unless he can invent a new and suggestive name for his friend's pleasure-craft? The foundation of the horse-yacht--if a thing that floats may be called fundamental--is a flat-bottomed boat, some fifty feet long and ten feet wide, with a draft of about eight inches. The deck is open for fifteen feet aft of the place where the bowsprit ought to be; behind that it is completely covered by a house, cabin, cottage, or whatever you choose to call it, with straight sides and a peaked roof of a very early Gothic pattern. Looking in at the door you see, first of all, two cots, one on either side of the passage; then an open space with a dining-table, a stove, and some chairs; beyond that a pantry with shelves, and a great chest for provisions. A door at the back opens into the kitchen, and from that another door opens into a sleeping-room for the boatmen. A huge wooden tiller curves over the stern of the boat, and the helmsman stands upon the kitchen-roof. Two canoes are floating behind, holding back, at the end of their long tow-ropes, as if reluctant to follow so clumsy a leader. This is an accurate description of the horse-yacht. If necessary it could be sworn to before a notary public. But I am perfectly sure that you might read this page through without skipping a word, and if you had never seen the creature with your own eyes, you would have no idea how absurd it looks and how comfortable it is.

While we were stowing away our trunks and bags under the cots, and making an equitable division of the hooks upon the walls, the motive power of the yacht stood patiently upon the shore, stamping a hoof, now and then, or shaking a shaggy head in mild protest against the flies. Three more pessimistic-looking horses I never saw. They were harnessed abreast, and fastened by a prodigious tow-rope to a short post in the middle of the forward deck. Their driver was a truculent, brigandish, bearded old fellow in long boots, a blue flannel shirt, and a black sombrero. He sat upon the middle horse, and some wild instinct of colour had made him tie a big red handkerchief around his shoulders, so that the eye of the beholder took delight in him. He posed like a bold, bad robber- chief. But in point of fact I believe he was the mildest and most inoffensive of men. We never heard him say anything except at a distance, to his horses, and we did not inquire what that was.

Well, as I have said, we were haggling courteously over those hooks in the cabin, when the boat gave a lurch. The bow swung out into the stream. There was a scrambling and clattering of iron horse- shoes on the rough shingle of the bank; and when we looked out of doors, our house was moving up the river with the boat under it.

The Ristigouche is a noble stream, stately and swift and strong. It rises among the dense forests in the northern part of New Brunswick--a moist upland region, of never-failing springs and innumerous lakes--and pours a flood of clear, cold water one hundred and fifty miles northward and eastward through the hills into the head of the Bay of Chaleurs. There are no falls in its course, but rapids everywhere. It is steadfast but not impetuous, quick but not turbulent, resolute and eager in its desire to get to the sea, like the life of a man who has a purpose

"Too great for haste, too high for rivalry."

The wonder is where all the water comes from. But the river is fed by more than six thousand square miles of territory. From both sides the little brooks come dashing in with their supply. At intervals a larger stream, reaching away back among the mountains like a hand with many fingers to gather

"The filtered tribute of the rough woodland,"

delivers its generous offering to the main current.

The names of the chief tributaries of the Ristigouche are curious. There is the headstrong Metapedia, and the crooked Upsalquitch, and the Patapedia, and the Quatawamkedgwick. These are words at which the tongue balks at first, but you soon grow used to them and learn to take anything of five syllables with a rush, as a hunter takes a five-barred gate, trusting to fortune that you will come down with the accent in the right place.

For six or seven miles above Metapedia the river has a breadth of about two hundred yards, and the valley slopes back rather gently to the mountains on either side. There is a good deal of cultivated land, and scattered farm-houses appear. The soil is excellent. But it is like a pearl cast before an obstinate, unfriendly climate. Late frosts prolong the winter. Early frosts curtail the summer. The only safe crops are grass, oats, and potatoes. And for half the year all the cattle must be housed and fed to keep them alive. This lends a melancholy aspect to agriculture. Most of the farmers look as if they had never seen better days. With few exceptions they are what a New Englander would call "slack-twisted and shiftless." Their barns are pervious to the weather, and their fences fail to connect. Sleds and ploughs rust together beside the house, and chickens scratch up the front-door yard. In truth, the people have been somewhat demoralised by the conflicting claims of different occupations; hunting in the fall, lumbering in the winter and spring, and working for the American sportsmen in the brief angling season, are so much more attractive and offer so much larger returns of ready money, that the tedious toil of farming is neglected. But for all that, in the bright days of midsummer, these green fields sloping down to the water, and pastures high up among the trees on the hillsides, look pleasant from a distance, and give an inhabited air to the landscape.

At the mouth of the Upsalquitch we passed the first of the fishing- lodges. It belongs to a sage angler from Albany who saw the beauty of the situation, years ago, and built a habitation to match it. Since that time a number of gentlemen have bought land fronting on good pools, and put up little cottages of a less classical style than Charles Cotton's "Fisherman's Retreat" on the banks of the river Dove, but better suited to this wild scenery, and more convenient to live in. The prevailing pattern is a very simple one; it consists of a broad piazza with a small house in the middle of it. The house bears about the same proportion to the piazza that the crown of a Gainsborough hat does to the brim. And the cost of the edifice is to the cost of the land as the first price of a share in a bankrupt railway is to the assessments which follow the reorganisation. All the best points have been sold, and real estate on the Ristigouche has been bid up to an absurd figure. In fact, the river is over-populated and probably over-fished. But we could hardly find it in our hearts to regret this, for it made the upward trip a very sociable one. At every lodge that was open, Favonius (who knows everybody) had a friend, and we must slip ashore in a canoe to leave the mail and refresh the inner man.

An angler, like an Arab, regards hospitality as a religious duty. There seems to be something in the craft which inclines the heart to kindness and good-fellowship. Few anglers have I seen who were not pleasant to meet, and ready to do a good turn to a fellow- fisherman with the gift of a killing fly or the loan of a rod. Not their own particular and well-proved favourite, of course, for that is a treasure which no decent man would borrow; but with that exception the best in their store is at the service of an accredited brother. One of the Ristigouche proprietors I remember, whose name bespoke him a descendant of Caledonia's patron saint. He was fishing in front of his own door when we came up, with our splashing horses, through the pool; but nothing would do but he must up anchor and have us away with him into the house to taste his good cheer. And there were his daughters with their books and needlework, and the photographs which they had taken pinned up on the wooden walls, among Japanese fans and bits of bright-coloured stuff in which the soul of woman delights, and, in a passive, silent way, the soul of man also. Then, after we had discussed the year's fishing, and the mysteries of the camera, and the deep question of what makes some negatives too thin and others too thick, we must go out to see the big salmon which one of the ladies had caught a few days before, and the large trout swimming about in their cold spring. It seemed to me, as we went on our way, that there could hardly be a more wholesome and pleasant summer-life for well-bred young women than this, or two amusements more innocent and sensible than photography and fly-fishing.

It must be confessed that the horse-yacht as a vehicle of travel is not remarkable in point of speed. Three miles an hour is not a very rapid rate of motion. But then, if you are not in a hurry, why should you care to make haste?

The wild desire to be forever racing against old Father Time is one of the kill-joys of modern life. That ancient traveller is sure to beat you in the long run, and as long as you are trying to rival him, he will make your life a burden. But if you will only acknowledge his superiority and profess that you do not approve of racing after all, he will settle down quietly beside you and jog along like the most companionable of creatures. That is a pleasant pilgrimage in which the journey itself is part of the destination.

As soon as one learns to regard the horse-yacht as a sort of moving house, it appears admirable. There is no dust or smoke, no rumble of wheels, or shriek of whistles. You are gliding along steadily through an ever-green world; skirting the silent hills; passing from one side of the river to the other when the horses have to swim the current to find a good foothold on the bank. You are on the water, but not at its mercy, for your craft is not disturbed by the heaving of rude waves, and the serene inhabitants do not say "I am sick." There is room enough to move about without falling overboard. You may sleep, or read, or write in your cabin, or sit upon the floating piazza in an arm-chair and smoke the pipe of peace, while the cool breeze blows in your face and the musical waves go singing down to the sea.

There was one feature about the boat, which commended itself very strongly to my mind. It was possible to stand upon the forward deck and do a little trout-fishing in motion. By watching your chance, when the corner of a good pool was within easy reach, you could send out a hasty line and cajole a sea-trout from his hiding- place. It is true that the tow-ropes and the post made the back cast a little awkward; and the wind sometimes blew the flies up on the roof of the cabin; but then, with patience and a short line the thing could be done. I remember a pair of good trout that rose together just as we were going through a boiling rapid; and it tried the strength of my split-bamboo rod to bring those fish to the net against the current and the motion of the boat.

When nightfall approached we let go the anchor (to wit, a rope tied to a large stone on the shore), ate our dinner "with gladness and singleness of heart" like the early Christians, and slept the sleep of the just, lulled by the murmuring of the waters, and defended from the insidious attacks of the mosquito by the breeze blowing down the river and the impregnable curtains over our beds. At daybreak, long before Favonius and I had finished our dreams, we were under way again; and when the trampling of the horses on some rocky shore wakened us, we could see the steep hills gliding past the windows and hear the rapids dashing against the side of the boat, and it seemed as if we were still dreaming.

At Cross Point, where the river makes a long loop around a narrow mountain, thin as a saw and crowned on its jagged edge by a rude wooden cross, we stopped for an hour to try the fishing. It was here that I hooked two mysterious creatures, each of which took the fly when it was below the surface, pulled for a few moments in a sullen way and then apparently melted into nothingness. It will always be a source of regret to me that the nature of these fish must remain unknown. While they were on the line it was the general opinion that they were heavy trout; but no sooner had they departed, than I became firmly convinced, in accordance with a psychological law which holds good all over the world, that they were both enormous salmon. Even the Turks have a proverb which says, "Every fish that escapes appears larger than it is." No one can alter that conviction, because no one can logically refute it. Our best blessings, like our largest fish, always depart before we have time to measure them.

The Slide Pool is in the wildest and most picturesque part of the river, about thirty-five miles above Metapedia. The stream, flowing swiftly down a stretch of rapids between forest-clad hills, runs straight toward the base of an eminence so precipitous that the trees can hardly find a foothold upon it, and seem to be climbing up in haste on either side of the long slide which leads to the summit. The current, barred by the wall of rock, takes a great sweep to the right, dashing up at first in angry waves, then falling away in oily curves and eddies, until at last it sleeps in a black deep, apparently almost motionless, at the foot of the hill. It was here, on the upper edge of the stream, opposite to the slide, that we brought our floating camp to anchor for some days. What does one do in such a watering-place?

Let us take a "specimen day." It is early morning, or to be more precise, about eight of the clock, and the white fog is just beginning to curl and drift away from the surface of the river. Sooner than this it would be idle to go out. The preternaturally early bird in his greedy haste may catch the worm; but the salmon never take the fly until the fog has lifted; and in this the scientific angler sees, with gratitude, a remarkable adaptation of the laws of nature to the tastes of man. The canoes are waiting at the front door. We step into them and push off, Favonius going up the stream a couple of miles to the mouth of the Patapedia, and I down, a little shorter distance, to the famous Indian House Pool. The slim boat glides easily on the current, with a smooth buoyant motion, quickened by the strokes of the paddles in the bow and the stern. We pass around two curves in the river and find ourselves at the head of the pool. Here the man in the stern drops the anchor, just on the edge of the bar where the rapid breaks over into the deeper water. The long rod is lifted; the fly unhooked from the reel; a few feet of line pulled through the rings, and the fishing begins.

First cast,--to the right, straight across the stream, about twenty feet: the current carries the fly down with a semicircular sweep, until it comes in line with the bow of the canoe. Second cast,--to the left, straight across the stream, with the same motion: the semicircle is completed, and the fly hangs quivering for a few seconds at the lowest point of the arc. Three or four feet of line are drawn from the reel. Third cast to the right; fourth cast to the left. Then a little more line. And so, with widening half- circles, the water is covered, gradually and very carefully, until at length the angler has as much line out as his two-handed rod can lift and swing. Then the first "drop" is finished; the man in the stern quietly pulls up the anchor and lets the boat drift down a few yards; the same process is repeated on the second drop; and so on, until the end of the run is reached and the fly has passed over all the good water. This seems like a very regular and somewhat mechanical proceeding as one describes it, but in the performance it is rendered intensely interesting by the knowledge that at any moment it is liable to be interrupted.

This morning the interruption comes early. At the first cast of the second drop, before the fly has fairly lit, a great flash of silver darts from the waves close by the boat. Usually a salmon takes the fly rather slowly, carrying it under water before he seizes it in his mouth. But this one is in no mood for deliberation. He has hooked himself with a rush, and the line goes whirring madly from the reel as he races down the pool. Keep the point of the rod low; he must have his own way now. Up with the anchor quickly, and send the canoe after him, bowman and sternman paddling with swift strokes. He has reached the deepest water; he stops to think what has happened to him; we have passed around and below him; and now, with the current to help us, we can begin to reel in. Lift the point of the rod, with a strong, steady pull. Put the force of both arms into it. The tough wood will stand the strain. The fish must be moved; he must come to the boat if he is ever to be landed. He gives a little and yields slowly to the pressure. Then suddenly he gives too much, and runs straight toward us. Reel in now as swiftly as possible, or else he will get a slack on the line and escape. Now he stops, shakes his head from side to side, and darts away again across the pool, leaping high out of water. Don't touch the reel! Drop the point of the rod quickly, for if he falls on the leader he will surely break it. Another leap, and another! Truly he is "a merry one," and it will go hard with us to hold him. But those great leaps have exhausted his strength, and now he follows the rod more easily. The men push the boat back to the shallow side of the pool until it touches lightly on the shore. The fish comes slowly in, fighting a little and making a few short runs; he is tired and turns slightly on his side; but even yet he is a heavy weight on the line, and it seems a wonder that so slight a thing as the leader can guide and draw him. Now he is close to the boat. The boatman steps out on a rock with his gaff. Steadily now and slowly, lift the rod, bending it backward. A quick sure stroke of the steel! a great splash! and the salmon is lifted upon the shore. How he flounces about on the stones. Give him the coup de grace at once, for his own sake as well as for ours. And now look at him, as he lies there on the green leaves. Broad back; small head tapering to a point; clean, shining sides with a few black spots on them; it is a fish fresh- run from the sea, in perfect condition, and that is the reason why he has given such good sport.

We must try for another before we go back. Again fortune favours us, and at eleven o'clock we pole up the river to the camp with two good salmon in the canoe. Hardly have we laid them away in the ice-box, when Favonius comes dropping down from Patapedia with three fish, one of them a twenty-four pounder. And so the morning's work is done.

In the evening, after dinner, it was our custom to sit out on the deck, watching the moonlight as it fell softly over the black hills and changed the river into a pale flood of rolling gold. The fragrant wreaths of smoke floated lazily away on the faint breeze of night. There was no sound save the rushing of the water and the crackling of the camp-fire on the shore. We talked of many things in the heavens above, and the earth beneath, and the waters under the earth; touching lightly here and there as the spirit of vagrant converse led us. Favonius has the good sense to talk about himself occasionally and tell his own experience. The man who will not do that must always be a dull companion. Modest egoism is the salt of conversation: you do not want too much of it; but if it is altogether omitted, everything tastes flat. I remember well the evening when he told me the story of the Sheep of the Wilderness.

"I was ill that summer," said he, "and the doctor had ordered me to go into the woods, but on no account to go without plenty of fresh meat, which was essential to my recovery. So we set out into the wild country north of Georgian Bay, taking a live sheep with us in order to be sure that the doctor's prescription might be faithfully followed. It was a young and innocent little beast, curling itself up at my feet in the canoe, and following me about on shore like a dog. I gathered grass every day to feed it, and carried it in my arms over the rough portages. It ate out of my hand and rubbed its woolly head against my leggings. To my dismay, I found that I was beginning to love it for its own sake and without any ulterior motives. The thought of killing and eating it became more and more painful to me, until at length the fatal fascination was complete, and my trip became practically an exercise of devotion to that sheep. I carried it everywhere and ministered fondly to its wants. Not for the world would I have alluded to mutton in its presence. And when we returned to civilisation I parted from the creature with sincere regret and the consciousness that I had humoured my affections at the expense of my digestion. The sheep did not give me so much as a look of farewell, but fell to feeding on the grass beside the farm-house with an air of placid triumph."

After hearing this touching tale, I was glad that no great intimacy had sprung up between Favonius and the chickens which we carried in a coop on the forecastle head, for there is no telling what restrictions his tender-heartedness might have laid upon our larder. But perhaps a chicken would not have given such an opening for misplaced affection as a sheep. There is a great difference in animals in this respect. I certainly never heard of any one falling in love with a salmon in such a way as to regard it as a fond companion. And this may be one reason why no sensible person who has tried fishing has ever been able to see any cruelty in it.

Suppose the fish is not caught by an angler, what is his alternative fate? He will either perish miserably in the struggles of the crowded net, or die of old age and starvation like the long, lean stragglers which are sometimes found in the shallow pools, or be devoured by a larger fish, or torn to pieces by a seal or an otter. Compared with any of these miserable deaths, the fate of a salmon who is hooked in a clear stream and after a glorious fight receives the happy despatch at the moment when he touches the shore, is a sort of euthanasia. And, since the fish was made to be man's food, the angler who brings him to the table of destiny in the cleanest, quickest, kindest way is, in fact, his benefactor.

There were some days, however, when our benevolent intentions toward the salmon were frustrated; mornings when they refused to rise, and evenings when they escaped even the skilful endeavours of Favonius. In vain did he try every fly in his book, from the smallest "Silver Doctor" to the largest "Golden Eagle." The "Black Dose" would not move them. The "Durham Ranger" covered the pool in vain. On days like this, if a stray fish rose, it was hard to land him, for he was usually but slightly hooked.

I remember one of these shy creatures which led me a pretty dance at the mouth of Patapedia. He came to the fly just at dusk, rising very softly and quietly, as if he did not really care for it but only wanted to see what it was like. He went down at once into deep water, and began the most dangerous and exasperating of all salmon-tactics, moving around in slow circles and shaking his head from side to side, with sullen pertinacity. This is called "jigging," and unless it can be stopped, the result is fatal.

I could not stop it. That salmon was determined to jig. He knew more than I did.

The canoe followed him down the pool. He jigged away past all three of the inlets of the Patapedia, and at last, in the still, deep water below, after we had laboured with him for half an hour, and brought him near enough to see that he was immense, he calmly opened his mouth and the fly came back to me void. That was a sad evening, in which all the consolations of philosophy were needed.

Sunday was a very peaceful day in our camp. In the Dominion of Canada, the question "to fish or not to fish" on the first day of the week is not left to the frailty of the individual conscience. The law on the subject is quite explicit, and says that between six o'clock on Saturday evening and six o'clock on Monday morning all nets shall be taken up and no one shall wet a line. The Ristigouche Salmon Club has its guardians stationed all along the river, and they are quite as inflexible in seeing that their employers keep this law as the famous sentinel was in refusing to let Napoleon pass without the countersign. But I do not think that these keen sportsmen regard it as a hardship; they are quite willing that the fish should have "an off day" in every week, and only grumble because some of the net-owners down at the mouth of the river have brought political influence to bear in their favour and obtained exemption from the rule. For our part, we were nothing loath to hang up our rods, and make the day different from other days.

In the morning we had a service in the cabin of the boat, gathering a little congregation of guardians and boatmen, and people from a solitary farm-house by the river. They came in pirogues--long, narrow boats hollowed from the trunk of a tree; the black-eyed, brown-faced girls sitting back to back in the middle of the boat, and the men standing up bending to their poles. It seemed a picturesque way of travelling, although none too safe.

In the afternoon we sat on deck and looked at the water. What a charm there is in watching a swift stream! The eye never wearies of following its curls and eddies, the shadow of the waves dancing over the stones, the strange, crinkling lines of sunlight in the shallows. There is a sort of fascination in it, lulling and soothing the mind into a quietude which is even pleasanter than sleep, and making it almost possible to do that of which we so often speak, but which we never quite accomplish--"think about nothing." Out on the edge of the pool, we could see five or six huge salmon, moving slowly from side to side, or lying motionless like gray shadows. There was nothing to break the silence except the thin clear whistle of the white-throated sparrow far back in the woods. This is almost the only bird-song that one hears on the river, unless you count the metallic "chr-r-r-r" of the kingfisher as a song.

Every now and then one of the salmon in the pool would lazily roll out of water, or spring high into the air and fall back with a heavy splash. What is it that makes salmon leap? Is it pain or pleasure? Do they do it to escape the attack of another fish, or to shake off a parasite that clings to them, or to practise jumping so that they can ascend the falls when they reach them, or simply and solely out of exuberant gladness and joy of living? Any one of these reasons would be enough to account for it on week-days. On Sunday I am quite sure they do it for the trial of the fisherman's faith.

But how should I tell all the little incidents which made that lazy voyage so delightful? Favonius was the ideal host, for on water, as well as on land, he knows how to provide for the liberty as well as for the wants of his guests. He understands also the fine art of conversation, which consists of silence as well as speech. And when it comes to angling, Izaak Walton himself could not have been a more profitable teacher by precept or example. Indeed, it is a curious thought, and one full of sadness to a well-constituted mind, that on the Ristigouche "I. W." would have been at sea, for the beloved father of all fishermen passed through this world without ever catching a salmon. So ill does fortune match with merit here below.

At last the days of idleness were ended. We could not

"Fold our tents like the Arabs, and as silently steal away;"

but we took down the long rods, put away the heavy reels, made the canoes fast to the side of the house, embarked the three horses on the front deck, and then dropped down with the current, swinging along through the rapids, and drifting slowly through the still places, now grounding on a hidden rock, and now sweeping around a sharp curve, until at length we saw the roofs of Metapedia and the ugly bridge of the railway spanning the river. There we left our floating house, awkward and helpless, like some strange relic of the flood, stranded on the shore. And as we climbed the bank we looked back and wondered whether Noah was sorry when he said good- bye to his ark.

1888.

ALPENROSEN AND GOAT'S MILK

Nay, let me tell you, there be many that have forty times our estates, that would give the greatest part of it to be healthful and cheerful like us; who, with the expense of a little money, have ate, and drank, and laughed, and angled, and sung, and slept securely; and rose next day, and cast away care, and sung, and laughed, and angled again; which are blessings rich men cannot purchase with all their money."--IZAAK WALTON: The Complete Angler.

A great deal of the pleasure of life lies in bringing together things which have no connection. That is the secret of humour--at least so we are told by the philosophers who explain the jests that other men have made--and in regard to travel, I am quite sure that it must be illogical in order to be entertaining. The more contrasts it contains, the better.

Perhaps it was some philosophical reflection of this kind that brought me to the resolution, on a certain summer day, to make a little journey, as straight as possible, from the sea-level streets of Venice to the lonely, lofty summit of a Tyrolese mountain, called, for no earthly reason that I can discover, the Gross- Venediger.

But apart from the philosophy of the matter, which I must confess to passing over very superficially at the time, there were other and more cogent reasons for wanting to go from Venice to the Big Venetian. It was the first of July, and the city on the sea was becoming tepid. A slumbrous haze brooded over canals and palaces and churches. It was difficult to keep one's conscience awake to Baedeker and a sense of moral obligation; Ruskin was impossible, and a picture-gallery was a penance. We floated lazily from one place to another, and decided that, after all, it was too warm to go in. The cries of the gondoliers, at the canal corners, grew more and more monotonous and dreamy. There was danger of our falling fast asleep and having to pay by the hour for a day's repose in a gondola. If it grew much warmer, we might be compelled to stay until the following winter in order to recover energy enough to get away. All the signs of the times pointed northward, to the mountains, where we should see glaciers and snow-fields, and pick Alpenrosen, and drink goat's milk fresh from the real goat.

I.

The first stage on the journey thither was by rail to Belluno-- about four or five hours. It is a sufficient commentary on railway travel that the most important thing about it is to tell how many hours it takes to get from one place to another.

We arrived in Belluno at night, and when we awoke the next morning we found ourselves in a picturesque little city of Venetian aspect, with a piazza and a campanile and a Palladian cathedral, surrounded on all sides by lofty hills. We were at the end of the railway and at the beginning of the Dolomites.

Although I have a constitutional aversion to scientific information given by unscientific persons, such as clergymen and men of letters, I must go in that direction far enough to make it clear that the word Dolomite does not describe a kind of fossil, nor a sect of heretics, but a formation of mountains lying between the Alps and the Adriatic. Draw a diamond on the map, with

Brixen at the northwest corner, Lienz at the northeast, Belluno at the southeast, and Trent at the southwest, and you will have included the region of the Dolomites, a country so picturesque, so interesting, so full of sublime and beautiful scenery, that it is equally a wonder and a blessing that it has not been long since completely overrun by tourists and ruined with railways. It is true, the glaciers and snowfields are limited; the waterfalls are comparatively few and slender, and the rivers small; the loftiest peaks are little more than ten thousand feet high. But, on the other hand, the mountains are always near, and therefore always imposing. Bold, steep, fantastic masses of naked rock, they rise suddenly from the green and flowery valleys in amazing and endless contrast; they mirror themselves in the tiny mountain lakes like pictures in a dream.

I believe the guide-book says that they are formed of carbonate of lime and carbonate of magnesia in chemical composition; but even if this be true, it need not prejudice any candid observer against them. For the simple and fortunate fact is that they are built of such stone that wind and weather, keen frost and melting snow and rushing water have worn and cut and carved them into a thousand shapes of wonder and beauty. It needs but little fancy to see in them walls and towers, cathedrals and campaniles, fortresses and cities, tinged with many hues from pale gray to deep red, and shining in an air so soft, so pure, so cool, so fragrant, under a sky so deep and blue and a sunshine so genial, that it seems like the happy union of Switzerland and Italy.

The great highway through this region from south to north is the Ampezzo road, which was constructed in 1830, along the valleys of the Piave, the Boite, and the Rienz--the ancient line of travel and commerce between Venice and Innsbruck. The road is superbly built, smooth and level. Our carriage rolled along so easily that we forgot and forgave its venerable appearance and its lack of accommodation for trunks. We had been persuaded to take four horses, as our luggage seemed too formidable for a single pair. But in effect our concession to apparent necessity turned out to be a mere display of superfluous luxury, for the two white leaders did little more than show their feeble paces, leaving the gray wheelers to do the work. We had the elevating sense of traveling four-in- hand, however--a satisfaction to which I do not believe any human being is altogether insensible.

At Longarone we breakfasted for the second time, and entered the narrow gorge of the Piave. The road was cut out of the face of the rock. Below us the long lumber-rafts went shooting down the swift river. Above, on the right, were the jagged crests of Monte Furlon and Premaggiore, which seemed to us very wonderful, because we had not yet learned how jagged the Dolomites can be. At Perarolo, where the Boite joins the Piave, there is a lump of a mountain in the angle between the rivers, and around this we crawled in long curves until we had risen a thousand feet, and arrived at the same Hotel Venezia, where we were to dine.

While dinner was preparing, the Deacon and I walked up to Pieve di Cadore, the birthplace of Titian. The house in which the great painter first saw the colours of the world is still standing, and tradition points out the very room in which he began to paint. I am not one of those who would inquire too closely into such a legend as this. The cottage may have been rebuilt a dozen times since Titian's day; not a scrap of the original stone or plaster may remain; but beyond a doubt the view that we saw from the window is the same that Titian saw. Now, for the first time, I could understand and appreciate the landscape-backgrounds of his pictures. The compact masses of mountains, the bold, sharp forms, the hanging rocks of cold gray emerging from green slopes, the intense blue aerial distances--these all had seemed to be unreal and imaginary--compositions of the studio. But now I knew that, whether Titian painted out-of-doors, like our modern impressionists, or not, he certainly painted what he had seen, and painted it as it is.

The graceful brown-eyed boy who showed us the house seemed also to belong to one of Titian's pictures. As we were going away, the Deacon, for lack of copper, rewarded him with a little silver piece, a half-lira, in value about ten cents. A celestial rapture of surprise spread over the child's face, and I know not what blessings he invoked upon us. He called his companions to rejoice with him, and we left them clapping their hands and dancing.

Driving after one has dined has always a peculiar charm. The motion seems pleasanter, the landscape finer than in the morning hours. The road from Cadore ran on a high level, through sloping pastures, white villages, and bits of larch forest. In its narrow bed, far below, the river Boite roared as gently as Bottom's lion. The afternoon sunlight touched the snow-capped pinnacle of Antelao and the massive pink wall of Sorapis on the right; on the left, across the valley, Monte Pelmo's vast head and the wild crests of La Rochetta and

Formin rose dark against the glowing sky. The peasants lifted their hats as we passed, and gave us a pleasant evening greeting. And so, almost without knowing it, we slipped out of Italy into Austria, and drew up before a bare, square stone building with the double black eagle, like a strange fowl split for broiling, staring at us from the wall, and an inscription to the effect that this was the Royal and Imperial Austrian Custom-house.

The officer saluted us so politely that we felt quite sorry that his duty required him to disturb our luggage. "The law obliged him to open one trunk; courtesy forbade him to open more." It was quickly done; and, without having to make any contribution to the income of His Royal and Imperial Majesty, Francis Joseph, we rolled on our way, through the hamlets of Acqua Bona and Zuel, into the Ampezzan metropolis of Cortina, at sundown.

The modest inn called "The Star of Gold" stood facing the public square, just below the church, and the landlady stood facing us in the doorway, with an enthusiastic welcome--altogether a most friendly and entertaining landlady, whose one desire in life seemed to be that we should never regret having chosen her house instead of "The White Cross," or "The Black Eagle."

"O ja!" she had our telegram received; and would we look at the rooms? Outlooking on the piazza, with a balcony from which we could observe the Festa of to-morrow. She hoped they would please us. "Only come in; accommodate yourselves."

It was all as she promised; three little bedrooms, and a little salon opening on a little balcony; queer old oil-paintings and framed embroideries and tiles hanging on the walls; spotless curtains, and board floors so white that it would have been a shame to eat off them without spreading a cloth to keep them from being soiled.

"These are the rooms of the Baron Rothschild when he comes here always in the summer--with nine horses and nine servants--the Baron Rothschild of Vienna."

I assured her that we did not know the Baron, but that should make no difference. We would not ask her to reduce the price on account of a little thing like that.

She did not quite grasp this idea, but hoped that we would not find the pension too dear at a dollar and fifty-seven and a half cents a day each, with a little extra for the salon and the balcony. "The English people all please themselves here--there comes many every summer--English Bishops and their families."

I inquired whether there were many Bishops in the house at that moment.

"No, just at present--she was very sorry--none."

"Well, then," I said, "it is all right. We will take the rooms."

Good Signora Barbaria, you did not speak the American language, nor understand those curious perversions of thought which pass among the Americans for humour; but you understood how to make a little inn cheerful and home-like; yours was a very simple and agreeable art of keeping a hotel. As we sat in the balcony after supper, listening to the capital playing of the village orchestra, and the Tyrolese songs with which they varied their music, we thought within ourselves that we were fortunate to have fallen upon the Star of Gold.

II.

Cortina lies in its valley like a white shell that has rolled down into a broad vase of malachite. It has about a hundred houses and seven hundred inhabitants, a large church and two small ones, a fine stone campanile with excellent bells, and seven or eight little inns. But it is more important than its size would signify, for it is the capital of the district whose lawful title is Magnifica Comunita di Ampezzo--a name conferred long ago by the Republic of Venice. In the fifteenth century it was Venetian territory; but in 1516, under Maximilian I., it was joined to Austria; and it is now one of the richest and most prosperous communes of the Tyrol. It embraces about thirty-five hundred people, scattered in hamlets and clusters of houses through the green basin with its four entrances, lying between the peaks of Tofana, Cristallo, Sorapis, and Nuvolau. The well-cultivated grain fields and meadows, the smooth alps filled with fine cattle, the well-built houses with their white stone basements and balconies of dark brown wood and broad overhanging roofs, all speak of industry and thrift. But there is more than mere agricultural prosperity in this valley. There is a fine race of men and women--intelligent, vigorous, and with a strong sense of beauty. The outer walls of the annex of the Hotel Aquila Nera are covered with frescoes of marked power and originality, painted by the son of the innkeeper. The art schools of Cortina are famous for their beautiful work in gold and silver filigree, and wood-inlaying. There are nearly two hundred pupils in these schools, all peasants' children, and they produce results, especially in intarsia, which are admirable. The village orchestra, of which I spoke a moment ago, is trained and led by a peasant's son, who has never had a thorough musical education. It must have at least twenty-five members, and as we heard them at the Festa they seemed to play with extraordinary accuracy and expression.

This Festa gave us a fine chance to see the people of the Ampezzo all together. It was the annual jubilation of the district; and from all the outlying hamlets and remote side valleys, even from the neighbouring vales of Agordo and Auronzo, across the mountains, and from Cadore, the peasants, men and women and children, had come in to the Sagro at Cortina. The piazza--which is really nothing more than a broadening of the road behind the church--was quite thronged. There must have been between two and three thousand people.

The ceremonies of the day began with general church-going. The people here are honestly and naturally religious. I have seen so many examples of what can only be called "sincere and unaffected piety," that I cannot doubt it. The church, on Cortina's feast- day, was crowded to the doors with worshippers, who gave every evidence of taking part not only with the voice, but also with the heart, in the worship.

Then followed the public unveiling of a tablet, on the wall of the little Inn of the Anchor, to the memory of Giammaria Ghedini, the founder of the art- schools of Cortina. There was music by the band; and an oration by a native Demosthenes (who spoke in Italian so fluent that it ran through one's senses like water through a sluice, leaving nothing behind), and an original Canto sung by the village choir, with a general chorus, in which they called upon the various mountains to "re-echo the name of the beloved master John- Mary as a model of modesty and true merit," and wound up with--

"Hurrah for John-Mary! Hurrah for his art! Hurrah for all teachers as skilful as he! Hurrah for us all, who have now taken part In singing together in do . . re . . mi."

It was very primitive, and I do not suppose that the celebration was even mentioned in the newspapers of the great world; but, after all, has not the man who wins such a triumph as this in the hearts of his own people, for whom he has made labour beautiful with the charm of art, deserved better of fame than many a crowned monarch or conquering warrior? We should be wiser if we gave less glory to the men who have been successful in forcing their fellow-men to die, and more glory to the men who have been successful in teaching their fellow-men how to live.

But the Festa of Cortina did not remain all day on this high moral plane. In the afternoon came what our landlady called "allerlei Dummheiten." There was a grand lottery for the benefit of the Volunteer Fire Department. The high officials sat up in a green wooden booth in the middle of the square, and called out the numbers and distributed the prizes. Then there was a greased pole with various articles of an attractive character tied to a large hoop at the top--silk aprons, and a green jacket, and bottles of wine, and half a smoked pig, and a coil of rope, and a purse. The gallant firemen voluntarily climbed up the pole as far as they could, one after another, and then involuntarily slid down again exhausted, each one wiping off a little more of the grease, until at last the lucky one came who profited by his forerunners' labours, and struggled to the top to snatch the smoked pig. After that it was easy.

Such is success in this unequal world; the man who wipes off the grease seldom gets the prize.

Then followed various games, with tubs of water; and coins fastened to the bottom of a huge black frying-pan, to be plucked off with the lips; and pots of flour to be broken with sticks; so that the young lads of the village were ducked and blackened and powdered to an unlimited extent, amid the hilarious applause of the spectators. In the evening there was more music, and the peasants danced in the square, the women quietly and rather heavily, but the men with amazing agility, slapping the soles of their shoes with their hands, or turning cartwheels in front of their partners. At dark the festivities closed with a display of fireworks; there were rockets and bombs and pinwheels; and the boys had tiny red and blue lights which they held until their fingers were burned, just as boys do in America; and there was a general hush of wonder as a particularly brilliant rocket swished into the dark sky; and when it burst into a rain of serpents, the crowd breathed out its delight in a long-drawn "Ah-h-h-h!" just as the crowd does everywhere. We might easily have imagined ourselves at a Fourth of July celebration in Vermont, if it had not been for the costumes.

The men of the Ampezzo Valley have kept but little that is peculiar in their dress. Men are naturally more progressive than women, and therefore less picturesque. The tide of fashion has swept them into the international monotony of coat and vest and trousers-- pretty much the same, and equally ugly, all over the world. Now and then you may see a short jacket with silver buttons, or a pair of knee-breeches; and almost all the youths wear a bunch of feathers or a tuft of chamois' hair in their soft green hats. But the women of the Ampezzo--strong, comely, with golden brown complexions, and often noble faces--are not ashamed to dress as their grandmothers did. They wear a little round black felt hat with rolled rim and two long ribbons hanging down at the back. Their hair is carefully braided and coiled, and stuck through and through with great silver pins. A black bodice, fastened with silver clasps, is covered in front with the ends of a brilliant silk kerchief, laid in many folds around the shoulders. The white shirt-sleeves are very full and fastened up above the elbow with coloured ribbon. If the weather is cool, the women wear a short black jacket, with satin yoke and high puffed sleeves. But, whatever the weather may be, they make no change in the large, full dark skirts, almost completely covered with immense silk aprons, by preference light blue. It is not a remarkably brilliant dress, compared with that which one may still see in some districts of Norway or Sweden, but upon the whole it suits the women of the Ampezzo wonderfully.

For my part, I think that when a woman has found a dress that becomes her, it is a waste of time to send to Paris for a fashion- plate.

III.

When the excitement of the Festa had subsided, we were free to abandon ourselves to the excursions in which the neighbourhood of Cortina abounds, and to which the guide-book earnestly calls every right-minded traveller. A walk through the light-green shadows of the larch-woods to the tiny lake of Ghedina, where we could see all the four dozen trout swimming about in the clear water and catching flies; a drive to the Belvedere, where there are superficial refreshments above and profound grottos below; these were trifles, though we enjoyed them. But the great mountains encircling us on every side, standing out in clear view with that distinctness and completeness of vision which is one charm of the Dolomites, seemed to summon us to more arduous enterprises. Accordingly, the Deacon and I selected the easiest one, engaged a guide, and prepared for the ascent.

Monte Nuvolau is not a perilous mountain. I am quite sure that at my present time of life I should be unwilling to ascend a perilous mountain unless there were something extraordinarily desirable at the top, or remarkably disagreeable at the bottom. Mere risk has lost the attractions which it once had. As the father of a family I felt bound to abstain from going for amusement into any place which a Christian lady might not visit with propriety and safety. Our preparation for Nuvolau, therefore, did not consist of ropes, ice-irons, and axes, but simply of a lunch and two long sticks.

Our way led us, in the early morning, through the clustering houses of Lacedel, up the broad, green slope that faces Cortina on the west, to the beautiful Alp Pocol. Nothing could exceed the pleasure of such a walk in the cool of the day, while the dew still lies on the short, rich grass, and the myriads of flowers are at their brightest and sweetest. The infinite variety and abundance of the blossoms is a continual wonder. They are sown more thickly than the stars in heaven, and the rainbow itself does not show so many tints. Here they are mingled like the threads of some strange embroidery; and there again nature has massed her colours; so that one spot will be all pale blue with innumerable forget-me-nots, or dark blue with gentians; another will blush with the delicate pink of the Santa Lucia or the deeper red of the clover; and another will shine yellow as cloth of gold. Over all this opulence of bloom the larks were soaring and singing. I never heard so many as in the meadows about Cortina. There was always a sweet spray of music sprinkling down out of the sky, where the singers poised unseen. It was like walking through a shower of melody.

From the Alp Pocol, which is simply a fair, lofty pasture, we had our first full view of Nuvolau, rising bare and strong, like a huge bastion, from the dark fir-woods. Through these our way led onward now for seven miles, with but a slight ascent. Then turning off to the left we began to climb sharply through the forest. There we found abundance of the lovely Alpenrosen, which do not bloom on the lower ground. Their colour is a deep, glowing pink, and when a Tyrolese girl gives you one of these flowers to stick in the band of your hat, you may know that you have found favour in her eyes.

Through the wood the cuckoo was calling--the bird which reverses the law of good children, and insists on being heard, but not seen.

When the forest was at an end we found ourselves at the foot of an alp which sloped steeply up to the Five Towers of Averau. The effect of these enormous masses of rock, standing out in lonely grandeur, like the ruins of some forsaken habitation of giants, was tremendous. Seen from far below in the valley their form was picturesque and striking; but as we sat beside the clear, cold spring which gushes out at the foot of the largest tower, the Titanic rocks seemed to hang in the air above us as if they would overawe us into a sense of their majesty. We felt it to the full; yet none the less, but rather the more, could we feel at the same time the delicate and ethereal beauty of the fringed gentianella and the pale Alpine lilies scattered on the short turf beside us.

We had now been on foot about three hours and a half. The half hour that remained was the hardest. Up over loose, broken stones that rolled beneath our feet, up over great slopes of rough rock, up across little fields of snow where we paused to celebrate the Fourth of July with a brief snowball fight, up along a narrowing ridge with a precipice on either hand, and so at last to the summit, 8600 feet above the sea.

It is not a great height, but it is a noble situation. For Nuvolau is fortunately placed in the very centre of the Dolomites, and so commands a finer view than many a higher mountain. Indeed, it is not from the highest peaks, according to my experience, that one gets the grandest prospects, but rather from those of middle height, which are so isolated as to give a wide circle of vision, and from which one can see both the valleys and the summits. Monte Rosa itself gives a less imposing view than the Gorner Grat.

It is possible, in this world, to climb too high for pleasure.

But what a panorama Nuvolau gave us on that clear, radiant summer morning--a perfect circle of splendid sight! On one side we looked down upon the Five Towers; on the other, a thousand feet below, the Alps, dotted with the huts of the herdsmen, sloped down into the deep-cut vale of Agordo. Opposite to us was the enormous mass of Tofana, a pile of gray and pink and saffron rock. When we turned the other way, we faced a group of mountains as ragged as the crests of a line of fir-trees, and behind them loomed the solemn head of Pelmo. Across the broad vale of the Boite, Antelao stood beside Sorapis, like a campanile beside a cathedral, and Cristallo towered above the green pass of the Three Crosses. Through that opening we could see the bristling peaks of the Sextenthal. Sweeping around in a wider circle from that point, we saw, beyond the Durrenstein, the snow-covered pile of the Gross-Glockner; the crimson bastions of the Rothwand appeared to the north, behind Tofana; then the white slopes that hang far away above the Zillerthal; and, nearer, the Geislerspitze, like five fingers thrust into the air; behind that, the distant Oetzthaler Mountain, and just a single white glimpse of the highest peak of the Ortler by the Engadine; nearer still we saw the vast fortress of the Sella group and the red combs of the Rosengarten; Monte Marmolata, the Queen of the Dolomites, stood before us revealed from base to peak in a bridal dress of snow; and southward we looked into the dark rugged face of La Civetta, rising sheer out of the vale of Agordo, where the Lake of Alleghe slept unseen. It was a sea of mountains, tossed around us into a myriad of motionless waves, and with a rainbow of colours spread among their hollows and across their crests. The cliffs of rose and orange and silver gray, the valleys of deepest green, the distant shadows of purple and melting blue, and the dazzling white of the scattered snow-fields seemed to shift and vary like the hues on the inside of a shell. And over all, from peak to peak, the light, feathery clouds went drifting lazily and slowly, as if they could not leave a scene so fair.

There is barely room on the top of Nuvolau for the stone shelter- hut which a grateful Saxon baron has built there as a sort of votive offering for the recovery of his health among the mountains. As we sat within and ate our frugal lunch, we were glad that he had recovered his health, and glad that he had built the hut, and glad that we had come to it. In fact, we could almost sympathise in our cold, matter-of-fact American way with the sentimental German inscription which we read on the wall:--

Von Nuvolau's hohen Wolkenstufen Lass mich, Natur, durch deine Himmel rufen-- An deiner Brust gesunde, wer da krank! So wird zum Volkerdank mein Sachsendank.

We refrained, however, from shouting anything through Nature's heaven, but went lightly down, in about three hours, to supper in the Star of Gold.

IV.

When a stern necessity forces one to leave Cortina, there are several ways of departure. We selected the main highway for our trunks, but for ourselves the Pass of the Three Crosses; the Deacon and the Deaconess in a mountain waggon, and I on foot. It should be written as an axiom in the philosophy of travel that the easiest way is best for your luggage, and the hardest way is best for yourself.

All along the rough road up to the Pass, we had a glorious outlook backward over the Val d' Ampezzo, and when we came to the top, we looked deep down into the narrow Val Buona behind Sorapis. I do not know just when we passed the Austrian border, but when we came to Lake Misurina we found ourselves in Italy again. My friends went on down the valley to Landro, but I in my weakness, having eaten of the trout of the lake for dinner, could not resist the temptation of staying over-night to catch one for breakfast.

It was a pleasant failure. The lake was beautiful, lying on top of the mountain like a bit of blue sky, surrounded by the peaks of Cristallo, Cadino, and the Drei Zinnen. It was a happiness to float on such celestial waters and cast the hopeful fly. The trout were there; they were large; I saw them; they also saw me; but, alas! I could not raise them. Misurina is, in fact, what the Scotch call "a dour loch," one of those places which are outwardly beautiful, but inwardly so demoralised that the trout will not rise.

When we came ashore in the evening, the boatman consoled me with the story of a French count who had spent two weeks there fishing, and only caught one fish. I had some thoughts of staying thirteen days longer, to rival the count, but concluded to go on the next morning, over Monte Pian and the Cat's Ladder to Landro.

The view from Monte Pian is far less extensive than that from Nuvolau; but it has the advantage of being very near the wild jumble of the Sexten Dolomites. The Three Shoemakers and a lot more of sharp and ragged fellows are close by, on the east; on the west, Cristallo shows its fine little glacier, and Rothwand its crimson cliffs; and southward Misurina gives to the view a glimpse of water, without which, indeed, no view is complete. Moreover, the mountain has the merit of being, as its name implies, quite gentle. I met the Deacon and the Deaconess at the top, they having walked up from Landro. And so we crossed the boundary line together again, seven thousand feet above the sea, from Italy into Austria. There was no custom-house.

The way down, by the Cat's Ladder, I travelled alone. The path was very steep and little worn, but even on the mountain-side there was no danger of losing it, for it had been blazed here and there, on trees and stones, with a dash of blue paint. This is the work of the invaluable DOAV--which is, being interpreted, the German- Austrian Alpine Club. The more one travels in the mountains, the more one learns to venerate this beneficent society, for the shelter-huts and guide-posts it has erected, and the paths it has made and marked distinctly with various colours. The Germans have a genius for thoroughness. My little brown guide-book, for example, not only informed me through whose back yard I must go to get into a certain path, but it told me that in such and such a spot I should find quite a good deal (ziemlichviel) of Edelweiss, and in another a small echo; it advised me in one valley to take provisions and dispense with a guide, and in another to take a guide and dispense with provisions, adding varied information in regard to beer, which in my case was useless, for I could not touch it. To go astray under such auspices would be worse than inexcusable.

Landro we found a very different place from Cortina. Instead of having a large church and a number of small hotels, it consists entirely of one large hotel and a very tiny church. It does not lie in a broad, open basin, but in a narrow valley, shut in closely by the mountains. The hotel, in spite of its size, is excellent, and a few steps up the valley is one of the finest views in the Dolomites. To the east opens a deep, wild gorge, at the head of which the pinnacles of the Drei Zinnen are seen; to the south the Durrensee fills the valley from edge to edge, and reflects in its pale waters the huge bulk of Monte Cristallo. It is such a complete picture, so finished, so compact, so balanced, that one might think a painter had composed it in a moment of inspiration. But no painter ever laid such colours on his canvas as those which are seen here when the cool evening shadows have settled upon the valley, all gray and green, while the mountains shine above in rosy Alpenglow, as if transfigured with inward fire.

There is another lake, about three miles north of Landro, called the Toblacher See, and there I repaired the defeat of Misurina. The trout at the outlet, by the bridge, were very small, and while the old fisherman was endeavouring to catch some of them in his new net, which would not work, I pushed my boat up to the head of the lake, where the stream came in. The green water was amazingly clear, but the current kept the fish with their heads up stream; so that one could come up behind them near enough for a long cast, without being seen. As my fly lighted above them and came gently down with the ripple, I saw the first fish turn and rise and take it. A motion of the wrist hooked him, and he played just as gamely as a trout in my favourite Long Island pond. How different the colour, though, as he came out of the water. This fellow was all silvery, with light pink spots on his sides. I took seven of his companions, in weight some four pounds, and then stopped because the evening light was failing.

How pleasant it is to fish in such a place and at such an hour! The novelty of the scene, the grandeur of the landscape, lend a strange charm to the sport. But the sport itself is so familiar that one feels at home--the motion of the rod, the feathery swish of the line, the sight of the rising fish--it all brings back a hundred woodland memories, and thoughts of good fishing comrades, some far away across the sea, and, perhaps, even now sitting around the forest camp-fire in Maine or Canada, and some with whom we shall keep company no more until we cross the greater ocean into that happy country whither they have preceded us.

V.

Instead of going straight down the valley by the high road, a drive of an hour, to the railway in the Pusterthal, I walked up over the mountains to the east, across the Platzwiesen, and so down through the Pragserthal. In one arm of the deep fir-clad vale are the Baths of Alt-Prags, famous for having cured the Countess of Gorz of a violent rheumatism in the fifteenth century. It is an antiquated establishment, and the guests, who were walking about in the fields or drinking their coffee in the balcony, had a fifteenth century look about them--venerable but slightly ruinous. But perhaps that was merely a rheumatic result.

All the waggons in the place were engaged. It is strange what an aggravating effect this state of affairs has upon a pedestrian who is bent upon riding. I did not recover my delight in the scenery until I had walked about five miles farther, and sat down on the grass, beside a beautiful spring, to eat my lunch.

What is there in a little physical rest that has such magic to restore the sense of pleasure? A few moments ago nothing pleased you--the bloom was gone from the peach; but now it has come back again--you wonder and admire. Thus cheerful and contented I trudged up the right arm of the valley to the Baths of Neu-Prags, less venerable, but apparently more popular than Alt-Prags, and on beyond them, through the woods, to the superb Pragser-Wildsee, a lake whose still waters, now blue as sapphire under the clear sky, and now green as emerald under gray clouds, sleep encircled by mighty precipices. Could anything be a greater contrast with Venice? There the canals alive with gondolas, and the open harbour bright with many-coloured sails; here, the hidden lake, silent and lifeless, save when

"A leaping fish Sends through the tarn a lonely cheer."

Tired, and a little foot-sore, after nine hours' walking, I came into the big railway hotel at Toblach that night. There I met my friends again, and parted from them and the Dolomites the next day, with regret. For they were "stepping westward;" but in order to get to the Gross-Venediger I must make a detour to the east, through the Pusterthal, and come up through the valley of the Isel to the great chain of mountains called the Hohe Tauern.

At the junction of the Isel and the Drau lies the quaint little city of Lienz, with its two castles--the square, double-towered one in the town, now transformed into the offices of the municipality, and the huge mediaeval one on a hill outside, now used as a damp restaurant and dismal beer-cellar. I lingered at Lienz for a couple of days, in the ancient hostelry of the Post. The hallways were vaulted like a cloister, the walls were three feet thick, the kitchen was in the middle of the house on the second floor, so that I looked into it every time I came from my room, and ordered dinner direct from the cook. But, so far from being displeased with these peculiarities, I rather liked the flavour of them; and then, in addition, the landlady's daughter, who was managing the house, was a person of most engaging manners, and there was trout and grayling fishing in a stream near by, and the neighbouring church of Dolsach contained the beautiful picture of the Holy Family, which Franz Defregger painted for his native village.

The peasant women of Lienz have one very striking feature in their dress--a black felt hat with a broad, stiff brim and a high crown, smaller at the top than at the base. It looks a little like the traditional head-gear of the Pilgrim Fathers, exaggerated. There is a solemnity about it which is fatal to feminine beauty.

I went by the post-waggon, with two slow horses and ten passengers, fifteen miles up the Iselthal, to Windisch-Matrei, a village whose early history is lost in the mist of antiquity, and whose streets are pervaded with odours which must have originated at the same time with the village. One wishes that they also might have shared the fate of its early history. But it is not fair to expect too much of a small place, and Windisch-Matrei has certainly a beautiful situation and a good inn. There I took my guide--a wiry and companionable little man, whose occupation in the lower world was that of a maker and merchant of hats--and set out for the Pragerhutte, a shelter on the side of the Gross-Venediger.

The path led under the walls of the old Castle of Weissenstein, and then in steep curves up the cliff which blocks the head of the valley, and along a cut in the face of the rock, into the steep, narrow Tauernthal, which divides the Glockner group from the Venediger. How entirely different it was from the region of the Dolomites! There the variety of colour was endless and the change incessant; here it was all green grass and trees and black rocks, with glimpses of snow. There the highest mountains were in sight constantly; here they could only be seen from certain points in the valley. There the streams played but a small part in the landscape; here they were prominent, the main river raging and foaming through the gorge below, while a score of waterfalls leaped from the cliffs on either side and dashed down to join it.

The peasants, men, women and children, were cutting the grass in the perpendicular fields; the woodmen were trimming and felling the trees in the fir-forests; the cattle-tenders were driving their cows along the stony path, or herding them far up on the hillsides. It was a lonely scene, and yet a busy one; and all along the road was written the history of the perils and hardships of the life which now seemed so peaceful and picturesque under the summer sunlight.

These heavy crosses, each covered with a narrow, pointed roof and decorated with a rude picture, standing beside the path, or on the bridge, or near the mill--what do they mean? They mark the place where a human life has been lost, or where some poor peasant has been delivered from a great peril, and has set up a memorial of his gratitude.

Stop, traveller, as you pass by, and look at the pictures. They have little more of art than a child's drawing on a slate; but they will teach you what it means to earn a living in these mountains. They tell of the danger that lurks on the steep slopes of grass, where the mowers have to go down with ropes around their waists, and in the beds of the streams where the floods sweep through in the spring, and in the forests where the great trees fall and crush men like flies, and on the icy bridges where a slip is fatal, and on the high passes where the winter snowstorm blinds the eyes and benumbs the limbs of the traveller, and under the cliffs from which avalanches slide and rocks roll. They show you men and women falling from waggons, and swept away by waters, and overwhelmed in land-slips. In the corner of the picture you may see a peasant with the black cross above his head--that means death. Or perhaps it is deliverance that the tablet commemorates--and then you will see the miller kneeling beside his mill with a flood rushing down upon it, or a peasant kneeling in his harvest-field under an inky-black cloud, or a landlord beside his inn in flames, or a mother praying beside her sick children; and above appears an angel, or a saint, or the Virgin with her Child.

Read the inscriptions, too, in their quaint German. Some of them are as humourous as the epitaphs in New England graveyards. I remember one which ran like this:

Here lies Elias Queer, Killed in his sixtieth year; Scarce had he seen the light of day When a waggon-wheel crushed his life away.

And there is another famous one which says:

Here perished the honoured and virtuous maiden, G.V.

This tablet was erected by her only son.

But for the most part a glance at these Marterl und Taferl, which are so frequent on all the mountain-roads of the Tyrol, will give you a strange sense of the real pathos of human life. If you are a Catholic, you will not refuse their request to say a prayer for the departed; if you are a Protestant, at least it will not hurt you to say one for those who still live and suffer and toil among such dangers.

After we had walked for four hours up the Tauernthal, we came to the Matreier-Tauernhaus, an inn which is kept open all the year for the shelter of travellers over the high pass that crosses the mountain-range at this point, from north to south. There we dined. It was a bare, rude place, but the dish of juicy trout was garnished with flowers, each fish holding a big pansy in its mouth, and as the maid set them down before me she wished me "a good appetite," with the hearty old-fashioned Tyrolese courtesy which still survives in these remote valleys. It is pleasant to travel in a land where the manners are plain and good. If you meet a peasant on the road he says, "God greet you!" if you give a child a couple of kreuzers he folds his hands and says, "God reward you!" and the maid who lights you to bed says, "Goodnight, I hope you will sleep well!"

Two hours more of walking brought us through Ausser-gschloss and Inner-gschloss, two groups of herdsmen's huts, tenanted only in summer, at the head of the Tauernthal. Midway between them lies a little chapel, cut into the solid rock for shelter from the avalanches. This lofty vale is indeed rightly named; for it is shut off from the rest of the world. The portal is a cliff down which the stream rushes in foam and thunder. On either hand rises a mountain wall. Within, the pasture is fresh and green, sprinkled with Alpine roses, and the pale river flows swiftly down between the rows of dark wooden houses. At the head of the vale towers the Gross-Venediger, with its glaciers and snow-fields dazzling white against the deep blue heaven. The murmur of the stream and the tinkle of the cow-bells and the jodelling of the herdsmen far up the slopes, make the music for the scene.

The path from Gschloss leads straight up to the foot of the dark pyramid of the Kesselkopf, and then in steep endless zig-zags along the edge of the great glacier. I saw, at first, the pinnacles of ice far above me, breaking over the face of the rock; then, after an hour's breathless climbing, I could look right into the blue crevasses; and at last, after another hour over soft snow-fields and broken rocks, I was at the Pragerhut, perched on the shoulder of the mountain, looking down upon the huge river of ice.

It was a magnificent view under the clear light of evening. Here in front of us, the Venediger with all his brother-mountains clustered about him; behind us, across the Tauern, the mighty chain of the Glockner against the eastern sky.

This is the frozen world. Here the Winter, driven back into his stronghold, makes his last stand against the Summer, in perpetual conflict, retreating by day to the mountain-peak, but creeping back at night in frost and snow to regain a little of his lost territory, until at last the Summer is wearied out, and the Winter sweeps down again to claim the whole valley for his own.

VI.

In the Pragerhut I found mountain comfort. There were bunks along the wall of the guest-room, with plenty of blankets. There was good store of eggs, canned meats, and nourishing black bread. The friendly goats came bleating up to the door at nightfall to be milked. And in charge of all this luxury there was a cheerful peasant-wife with her brown-eyed daughter, to entertain travellers. It was a pleasant sight to see them, as they sat down to their supper with my guide; all three bowed their heads and said their "grace before meat," the guide repeating the longer prayer and the mother and daughter coming in with the responses. I went to bed with a warm and comfortable feeling about my heart. It was a good ending for the day. In the morning, if the weather remained clear, the alarm-clock was to wake us at three for the ascent to the summit.

But can it be three o'clock already. The gibbous moon still hangs in the sky and casts a feeble light over the scene. Then up and away for the final climb. How rough the path is among the black rocks along the ridge! Now we strike out on the gently rising glacier, across the crust of snow, picking our way among the crevasses, with the rope tied about our waists for fear of a fall. How cold it is! But now the gray light of morning dawns, and now the beams of sunrise shoot up behind the Glockner, and now the sun itself glitters into sight. The snow grows softer as we toil up the steep, narrow comb between the Gross-Venediger and his neighbour the Klein-Venediger. At last we have reached our journey's end. See, the whole of the Tyrol is spread out before us in wondrous splendour, as we stand on this snowy ridge; and at our feet the Schlatten glacier, like a long, white snake, curls down into the valley.

There is still a little peak above us; an overhanging horn of snow which the wind has built against the mountain-top. I would like to stand there, just for a moment. The guide protests it would be dangerous, for if the snow should break it would be a fall of a thousand feet to the glacier on the northern side. But let us dare the few steps upward. How our feet sink! Is the snow slipping? Look at the glacier! What is happening? It is wrinkling and curling backward on us, serpent-like. Its head rises far above us. All its icy crests are clashing together like the ringing of a thousand bells. We are falling! I fling out my arm to grasp the guide--and awake to find myself clutching a pillow in the bunk. The alarm-clock is ringing fiercely for three o'clock. A driving snow-storm is beating against the window. The ground is white. Peer through the clouds as I may, I cannot even catch a glimpse of the vanished Gross-Venediger.

1892.

AU LARGE

Wherever we strayed, the same tranquil leisure enfolded us; day followed day in an order unbroken and peaceful as the unfolding of the flowers and the silent march of the stars. Time no longer ran like the few sands in a delicate hour-glass held by a fragile human hand, but like a majestic river fed by fathomless seas. . . . We gave ourselves up to the sweetness of that unmeasured life, without thought of yesterday or to-morrow; we drank the cup to-day held to our lips, and knew that so long as we were athirst that draught would not be denied us." --HAMILTON W. MABIE: Under the Trees.

There is magic in words, surely, and many a treasure besides Ali Baba's is unlocked with a verbal key. Some charm in the mere sound, some association with the pleasant past, touches a secret spring. The bars are down; the gate open; you are made free of all the fields of memory and fancy--by a word.

Au large! Envoyez au large! is the cry of the Canadian voyageurs as they thrust their paddles against the shore and push out on the broad lake for a journey through the wilderness. Au large! is what the man in the bow shouts to the man in the stern when the birch canoe is running down the rapids, and the water grows too broken, and the rocks too thick, along the river-bank. Then the frail bark must be driven out into the very centre of the wild current, into the midst of danger to find safety, dashing, like a frightened colt, along the smooth, sloping lane bordered by white fences of foam.

Au large! When I hear that word, I hear also the crisp waves breaking on pebbly beaches, and the big wind rushing through innumerable trees, and the roar of headlong rivers leaping down the rocks, I see long reaches of water sparkling in the sun, or sleeping still between evergreen walls beneath a cloudy sky; and the gleam of white tents on the shore; and the glow of firelight dancing through the woods. I smell the delicate vanishing perfume of forest flowers; and the incense of rolls of birch-bark, crinkling and flaring in the camp-fire; and the soothing odour of balsam-boughs piled deep for woodland beds--the veritable and only genuine perfume of the land of Nod. The thin shining veil of the Northern lights waves and fades and brightens over the night sky; at the sound of the word, as at the ringing of a bell, the curtain rises. Scene, the Forest of Arden; enter a party of hunters.

It was in the Lake St. John country, two hundred miles north of Quebec, that I first heard my rustic incantation; and it seemed to fit the region as if it had been made for it. This is not a little pocket wilderness like the Adirondacks, but something vast and primitive. You do not cross it, from one railroad to another, by a line of hotels. You go into it by one river as far as you like, or dare; and then you turn and come back again by another river, making haste to get out before your provisions are exhausted. The lake itself is the cradle of the mighty Saguenay: an inland sea, thirty miles across and nearly round, lying in the broad limestone basin north of the Laurentian Mountains. The southern and eastern shores have been settled for twenty or thirty years; and the rich farm-land yields abundant crops of wheat and oats and potatoes to a community of industrious habitants, who live in little modern villages, named after the saints and gathered as closely as possible around big gray stone churches, and thank the good Lord that he has given them a climate at least four or five degrees milder than Quebec. A railroad, built through a region of granite hills, which will never be tamed to the plough, links this outlying settlement to the civilised world; and at the end of the railroad the Hotel Roberval, standing on a hill above the lake, offers to the pampered tourist electric lights, and spring-beds, and a wide veranda from which he can look out across the water into the face of the wilderness.

Northward and westward the interminable forest rolls away to the shores of Hudson's Bay and the frozen wastes of Labrador. It is an immense solitude. A score of rivers empty into the lake; little ones like the Pikouabi and La Pipe, and middle-sized ones like the Ouiatehouan and La Belle Riviere, and big ones like the Mistassini and the Peribonca; and each of these streams is the clue to a labyrinth of woods and waters. The canoe-man who follows it far enough will find himself among lakes that are not named on any map; he will camp on virgin ground, and make the acquaintance of unsophisticated fish; perhaps even, like the maiden in the fairy- tale, he will meet with the little bear, and the middle-sized bear, and the great big bear.

Damon and I set out on such an expedition shortly after the nodding lilies in the Connecticut meadows had rung the noon-tide bell of summer, and when the raspberry bushes along the line of the Quebec and Lake St. John Railway had spread their afternoon collation for birds and men. At Roberval we found our four guides waiting for us, and the steamboat took us all across the lake to the Island House, at the northeast corner. There we embarked our tents and blankets, our pots and pans, and bags of flour and potatoes and bacon and other delicacies, our rods and guns, and last, but not least, our axes (without which man in the woods is a helpless creature), in two birch-bark canoes, and went flying down the Grande Decharge.

It is a wonderful place, this outlet of Lake St. John. All the floods of twenty rivers are gathered here, and break forth through a net of islands in a double stream, divided by the broad Ile d'Alma, into the Grande Decharge and the Petite Decharge. The southern outlet is small, and flows somewhat more quietly at first. But the northern outlet is a huge confluence and tumult of waters. You see the set of the tide far out in the lake, sliding, driving, crowding, hurrying in with smooth currents and swirling eddies, toward the corner of escape. By the rocky cove where the Island House peers out through the fir-trees, the current already has a perceptible slope. It begins to boil over hidden stones in the middle, and gurgles at projecting points of rock. A mile farther down there is an islet where the stream quickens, chafes, and breaks into a rapid. Behind the islet it drops down in three or four foaming steps. On the outside it makes one long, straight rush into a line of white-crested standing waves.

As we approached, the steersman in the first canoe stood up to look over the course. The sea was high. Was it too high? The canoes were heavily loaded. Could they leap the waves? There was a quick talk among the guides as we slipped along, undecided which way to turn. Then the question seemed to settle itself, as most of these woodland questions do, as if some silent force of Nature had the casting-vote. "Sautez, sautez!" cried Ferdinand, "envoyez au large!" In a moment we were sliding down the smooth back of the rapid, directly toward the first big wave. The rocky shore went by us like a dream; we could feel the motion of the earth whirling around with us. The crest of the billow in front curled above the bow of the canoe. "Arret', arret', doucement!" A swift stroke of the paddle checked the canoe, quivering and prancing like a horse suddenly reined in. The wave ahead, as if surprised, sank and flattened for a second. The canoe leaped through the edge of it, swerved to one side, and ran gayly down along the fringe of the line of billows, into quieter water.

Every one feels the exhilaration of such a descent. I know a lady who almost cried with fright when she went down her first rapid, but before the voyage was ended she was saying:--

"Count that day lost whose low, descending sun Sees no fall leaped, no foaming rapid run."

It takes a touch of danger to bring out the joy of life.

Our guides began to shout, and joke each other, and praise their canoes.

"You grazed that villain rock at the corner," said Jean; "didn't you know where it was?"

"Yes, after I touched it," cried Ferdinand; "but you took in a bucket of water, and I suppose your m'sieu' is sitting on a piece of the river. Is it not?"

This seemed to us all a very merry jest, and we laughed with the same inextinguishable laughter which a practical joke, according to Homer, always used to raise in Olympus. It is one of the charms of life in the woods that it brings back the high spirits of boyhood and renews the youth of the world. Plain fun, like plain food, tastes good out-of-doors. Nectar is the sweet sap of a maple-tree. Ambrosia is only another name for well-turned flapjacks. And all the immortals, sitting around the table of golden cedar-slabs, make merry when the clumsy Hephaistos, playing the part of Hebe, stumbles over a root and upsets the plate of cakes into the fire.

The first little rapid of the Grande Decharge was only the beginning. Half a mile below we could see the river disappear between two points of rock. There was a roar of conflict, and a golden mist hanging in the air, like the smoke of battle. All along the place where the river sank from sight, dazzling heads of foam were flashing up and falling back, as if a horde of water-sprites were vainly trying to fight their way up to the lake. It was the top of the grande chute, a wild succession of falls and pools where no boat could live for a moment. We ran down toward it as far as the water served, and then turned off among the rocks on the left hand, to take the portage.

These portages are among the troublesome delights of a journey in the wilderness. To the guides they mean hard work, for everything, including the boats, must be carried on their backs. The march of the canoes on dry land is a curious sight. Andrew Marvell described it two hundred years ago when he was poetizing beside the little river Wharfe in Yorkshire:--

"And now the salmon-fishers moist Their leathern boats begin to hoist, And like antipodes in shoes Have shod their heads in their canoes. How tortoise-like, but none so slow, These rational amphibii go!"

But the sportsman carries nothing, except perhaps his gun, or his rod, or his photographic camera; and so for him the portage is only a pleasant opportunity to stretch his legs, cramped by sitting in the canoe, and to renew his acquaintance with the pretty things that are in the woods.

We sauntered along the trail, Damon and I, as if school were out and would never keep again. How fresh and tonic the forest seemed as we plunged into its bath of shade. There were our old friends the cedars, with their roots twisted across the path; and the white birches, so trim in youth and so shaggy in age; and the sociable spruces and balsams, crowding close together, and interlacing their arms overhead. There were the little springs, trickling through the moss; and the slippery logs laid across the marshy places; and the fallen trees, cut in two and pushed aside,--for this was a much-travelled portage.

Around the open spaces, the tall meadow-rue stood dressed in robes of fairy white and green. The blue banners of the fleur-de-lis were planted beside the springs. In shady corners, deeper in the wood, the fragrant pyrola lifted its scape of clustering bells, like a lily of the valley wandered to the forest. When we came to the end of the portage, a perfume like that of cyclamens in Tyrolean meadows welcomed us, and searching among the loose grasses by the water-side we found the exquisite purple spikes of the lesser fringed orchis, loveliest and most ethereal of all the woodland flowers save one. And what one is that? Ah, my friend, it is your own particular favourite, the flower, by whatever name you call it, that you plucked long ago when you were walking in the forest with your sweetheart,--

"Im wunderschonen Monat Mai Als alle Knospen sprangen."

We launched our canoes again on the great pool at the foot of the first fall,-- a broad sweep of water a mile long and half a mile wide, full of eddies and strong currents, and covered with drifting foam. There was the old campground on the point, where I had tented so often with my lady Greygown, fishing for ouananiche, the famous land-locked salmon of Lake St. John. And there were the big fish, showing their back fins as they circled lazily around in the eddies, as if they were waiting to play with us. But the goal of our day's journey was miles away, and we swept along with the stream, now through a rush of quick water, boiling and foaming, now through a still place like a lake, now through

"Fairy crowds Of islands, that together lie, As quietly as spots of sky Among the evening clouds."

The beauty of the shores was infinitely varied, and unspoiled by any sign of the presence of man. We met no company except a few king-fishers, and a pair of gulls who had come up from the sea to spend the summer, and a large flock of wild ducks, which the guides call "Betseys," as if they were all of the gentler sex. In such a big family of girls we supposed that a few would not be missed, and Damon bagged two of the tenderest for our supper.

In the still water at the mouth of the Riviere Mistook, just above the Rapide aux Cedres, we went ashore on a level wooded bank to make our first camp and cook our dinner. Let me try to sketch our men as they are busied about the fire.

They are all French Canadians of unmixed blood, descendants of the men who came to New France with Samuel de Champlain, that incomparable old woodsman and life-long lover of the wilderness. Ferdinand Larouche is our chef--there must be a head in every party for the sake of harmony--and his assistant is his brother Francois. Ferdinand is a stocky little fellow, a "sawed off" man, not more than five feet two inches tall, but every inch of him is pure vim. He can carry a big canoe or a hundred-weight of camp stuff over a mile portage without stopping to take breath. He is a capital canoe-man, with prudence enough to balance his courage, and a fair cook, with plenty of that quality which is wanting in the ordinary cook of commerce--good humour. Always joking, whistling, singing, he brings the atmosphere of a perpetual holiday along with him. His weather-worn coat covers a heart full of music. He has two talents which make him a marked man among his comrades. He plays the fiddle to the delight of all the balls and weddings through the country-side; and he speaks English to the admiration and envy of the other guides. But like all men of genius he is modest about his accomplishments. "H'I not spik good h'English--h'only for camp--fishin', cookin', dhe voyage--h'all dhose t'ings." The aspirates puzzle him. He can get though a slash of fallen timber more easily than a sentence full of "this" and "that." Sometimes he expresses his meaning queerly. He was telling me once about his farm, "not far off here, in dhe Riviere au Cochon, river of dhe pig, you call 'im. H'I am a widow, got five sons, t'ree of dhem are girls." But he usually ends by falling back into French, which, he assures you, you speak to perfection, "much better than the Canadians; the French of Paris in short--M'sieu' has been in Paris?" Such courtesy is born in the blood, and is irresistible. You cannot help returning the compliment and assuring him that his English is remarkable, good enough for all practical purposes, better than any of the other guides can speak. And so it is.

Francois is a little taller, a little thinner, and considerably quieter than Ferdinand. He laughs loyally at his brother's jokes, and sings the response to his songs, and wields a good second paddle in the canoe.

Jean--commonly called Johnny--Morel is a tall, strong man of fifty, with a bushy red beard that would do credit to a pirate. But when you look at him more closely, you see that he has a clear, kind blue eye and a most honest, friendly face under his slouch hat. He has travelled these woods and waters for thirty years, so that he knows the way through them by a thousand familiar signs, as well as you know the streets of the city. He is our pathfinder.

The bow paddle in his canoe is held by his son Joseph, a lad not quite fifteen, but already as tall, and almost as strong as a man. "He is yet of the youth," said Johnny, "and he knows not the affairs of the camp. This trip is for him the first--it is his school--but I hope he will content you. He is good, M'sieu', and of the strongest for his age. I have educated already two sons in the bow of my canoe. The oldest has gone to Pennsylvanie; he peels the bark there for the tanning of leather. The second had the misfortune of breaking his leg, so that he can no longer kneel to paddle. He has descended to the making of shoes. Joseph is my third pupil. And I have still a younger one at home waiting to come into my school."

A touch of family life like that is always refreshing, and doubly so in the wilderness. For what is fatherhood at its best, everywhere, but the training of good men to take the teacher's place when his work is done? Some day, when Johnny's rheumatism has made his joints a little stiffer and his eyes have lost something of their keenness, he will be wielding the second paddle in the boat, and going out only on the short and easy trips. It will be young Joseph that steers the canoe through the dangerous places, and carries the heaviest load over the portages, and leads the way on the long journeys.

It has taken me longer to describe our men than it took them to prepare our frugal meal: a pot of tea, the woodsman's favourite drink, (I never knew a good guide that would not go without whisky rather than without tea,) a few slices of toast and juicy rashers of bacon, a kettle of boiled potatoes, and a relish of crackers and cheese. We were in a hurry to be off for an afternoon's fishing, three or four miles down the river, at the Ile Maligne.

The island is well named, for it is the most perilous place on the river, and has a record of disaster and death. The scattered waters of the Discharge are drawn together here into one deep, narrow, powerful stream, flowing between gloomy shores of granite. In mid-channel the wicked island shows its scarred and bristling head, like a giant ready to dispute the passage. The river rushes straight at the rocky brow, splits into two currents, and raves away on both sides of the island in a double chain of furious falls and rapids.

In these wild waters we fished with immense delight and fair success, scrambling down among the huge rocks along the shore, and joining the excitement of an Alpine climb with the placid pleasures of angling. At nightfall we were at home again in our camp, with half a score of onananiche, weighing from one to four pounds each.

Our next day's journey was long and variegated. A portage of a mile or two across the Ile d'Alma, with a cart to haul our canoes and stuff, brought us to the Little Discharge, down which we floated for a little way, and then hauled through the village of St. Joseph to the foot of the Carcajou, or Wildcat Falls. A mile of quick water was soon passed, and we came to the junction of the Little Discharge with the Grand Discharge at the point where the picturesque club-house stands in a grove of birches beside the big Vache Caille Falls. It is lively work crossing the pool here, when the water is high and the canoes are heavy; but we went through the labouring seas safely, and landed some distance below, at the head of the Rapide Gervais, to eat our lunch. The water was too rough to run down with loaded boats, so Damon and I had to walk about three miles along the river-bank, while the men went down with the canoes.

On our way beside the rapids, Damon geologised, finding the marks of ancient glaciers, and bits of iron-ore, and pockets of sand full of infinitesimal garnets, and specks of gold washed from the primitive granite; and I fished, picking up a pair of ouananiche in foam-covered nooks among the rocks. The swift water was almost passed when we embarked again and ran down the last slope into a long deadwater.

The shores, at first bold and rough, covered with dense thickets of second-growth timber, now became smoother and more fertile. Scattered farms, with square, unpainted houses, and long, thatched barns, began to creep over the hills toward the river. There was a hamlet, called St. Charles, with a rude little church and a campanile of logs. The cure, robed in decent black and wearing a tall silk hat of the vintage of 1860, sat on the veranda of his trim presbytery, looking down upon us, like an image of propriety smiling at Bohemianism. Other craft appeared on the river. A man and his wife paddling an old dugout, with half a dozen children packed in amidships a crew of lumbermen, in a sharp-nosed bateau, picking up stray logs along the banks; a couple of boatloads of young people returning merrily from a holiday visit; a party of berry-pickers in a flat-bottomed skiff; all the life of the country-side was in evidence on the river. We felt quite as if we had been "in the swim" of society, when at length we reached the point where the Riviere des Aunes came tumbling down a hundred-foot ladder of broken black rocks. There we pitched our tents in a strip of meadow by the water-side, where we could have the sound of the falls for a slumber-song all night and the whole river for a bath at sunrise.

A sparkling draught of crystal weather was poured into our stirrup- cup in the morning, as we set out for a drive of fifteen miles across country to the Riviere a l'Ours, a tributary of the crooked, unnavigable river of Alders. The canoes and luggage were loaded on a couple of charrettes, or two-wheeled carts. But for us and the guides there were two quatre-roues, the typical vehicles of the century, as characteristic of Canada as the carriole is of Norway. It is a two-seated buckboard, drawn by one horse, and the back seat is covered with a hood like an old-fashioned poke bonnet. The road is of clay and always rutty. It runs level for a while, and then jumps up a steep ridge and down again, or into a deep gully and out again. The habitant's idea of good driving is to let his horse slide down the hill and gallop up. This imparts a spasmodic quality to the motion, like Carlyle's style.

The native houses are strung along the road. The modern pattern has a convex angle in the roof, and dormer-windows; it is a rustic adaptation of the Mansard. The antique pattern, which is far more picturesque, has a concave curve in the roof, and the eaves project like eyebrows, shading the flatness of the face. Paint is a rarity. The prevailing colour is the soft gray of weather-beaten wood. Sometimes, in the better class of houses, a gallery is built across the front and around one side, and a square of garden is fenced in, with dahlias and hollyhocks and marigolds, and perhaps a struggling rosebush, and usually a small patch of tobacco growing in one corner. Once in a long while you may see a balm-of-Gilead tree, or a clump of sapling poplars, planted near the door.

How much better it would have been if the farmer had left a few of the noble forest-trees to shade his house. But then, when the farmer came into the wilderness he was not a farmer, he was first of all a wood-chopper. He regarded the forest as a stubborn enemy in possession of his land. He attacked it with fire and axe and exterminated it, instead of keeping a few captives to hold their green umbrellas over his head when at last his grain fields should be smiling around him and he should sit down on his doorstep to smoke a pipe of home-grown tobacco.

In the time of adversity one should prepare for prosperity. I fancy there are a good many people unconsciously repeating the mistake of the Canadian farmer--chopping down all the native growths of life, clearing the ground of all the useless pretty things that seem to cumber it, sacrificing everything to utility and success. We fell the last green tree for the sake of raising an extra hill of potatoes; and never stop to think what an ugly, barren place we may have to sit in while we eat them. The ideals, the attachments--yes, even the dreams of youth are worth saving. For the artificial tastes with which age tries to make good their loss grow very slowly and cast but a slender shade.

Most of the Canadian farmhouses have their ovens out-of-doors. We saw them everywhere; rounded edifices of clay, raised on a foundation of logs, and usually covered with a pointed roof of boards. They looked like little family chapels--and so they were; shrines where the ritual of the good housewife was celebrated, and the gift of daily bread, having been honestly earned, was thankfully received.

At one house we noticed a curious fragment of domestic economy. Half a pig was suspended over the chimney, and the smoke of the summer fire was turned to account in curing the winter's meat. I guess the children of that family had a peculiar fondness for the parental roof-tree. We saw them making mud-pies in the road, and imagined that they looked lovingly up at the pendent porker, outlined against the sky,--a sign of promise, prophetic of bacon.

About noon the road passed beyond the region of habitation into a barren land, where blueberries were the only crop, and partridges took the place of chickens. Through this rolling gravelly plain, sparsely wooded and glowing with the tall magenta bloom of the fireweed, we drove toward the mountains, until the road went to seed and we could follow it no longer. Then we took to the water and began to pole our canoes up the River of the Bear. It was a clear, amber-coloured stream, not more than ten or fifteen yards wide, running swift and strong, over beds of sand and rounded pebbles. The canoes went wallowing and plunging up the narrow channel, between thick banks of alders, like clumsy sea-monsters. All the grace with which they move under the strokes of the paddle, in large waters, was gone. They looked uncouth and predatory, like a pair of seals that I once saw swimming far up the river Ristigouche in chase of fish. From the bow of each canoe the landing-net stuck out as a symbol of destruction--after the fashion of the Dutch admiral who nailed a broom to his masthead. But it would have been impossible to sweep the trout out of that little river by any fair method of angling, for there were millions of them; not large, but lively, and brilliant, and fat; they leaped in every bend of the stream. We trailed our flies, and made quick casts here and there, as we went along. It was fishing on the wing. And when we pitched our tents in a hurry at nightfall on the low shore of Lac Sale, among the bushes where firewood was scarce and there were no sapins for the beds, we were comforted for the poorness of the camp-ground by the excellence of the trout supper.

It was a bitter cold night for August. There was a skin of ice on the water-pail at daybreak. We were glad to be up and away for an early start. The river grew wilder and more difficult. There were rapids, and ruined dams built by the lumbermen years ago. At these places the trout were larger, and so plentiful that it was easy to hook two at a cast. It came on to rain furiously while we were eating our lunch. But we did not seem to mind it any more than the fish did. Here and there the river was completely blocked by fallen trees. The guides called it bouchee, "corked," and leaped out gayly into the water with their axes to "uncork" it. We passed through some pretty lakes, unknown to the map-makers, and arrived, before sundown, at the Lake of the Bear, where we were to spend a couple of days. The lake was full of floating logs, and the water, raised by the heavy rains and the operations of the lumbermen, was several feet above its usual level. Nature's landing-places were all blotted out, and we had to explore halfway around the shore before we could get out comfortably. We raised the tents on a small shoulder of a hill, a few rods above the water; and a glorious camp-fire of birch logs soon made us forget our misery as though it had not been.

The name of the Lake of the Beautiful Trout made us desire to visit it. The portage was said to be only fifty acres long (the arpent is the popular measure of distance here), but it passed over a ridge of newly burned land, and was so entangled with ruined woods and desolate of birds and flowers that it seemed to us at least five miles. The lake was charming--a sheet of singularly clear water, of a pale green tinge, surrounded by wooded hills. In the translucent depths trout and pike live together, but whether in peace or not I cannot tell. Both of them grow to an enormous size, but the pike are larger and have more capacious jaws. One of them broke my tackle and went off with a silver spoon in his mouth, as if he had been born to it. Of course the guides vowed that they saw him as he passed under the canoe, and declared that he must weigh thirty or forty pounds. The spectacles of regret always magnify.

The trout were coy. We took only five of them, perfect specimens of the true Salvelinus fontinalis, with square tails, and carmine spots on their dark, mottled sides; the largest weighed three pounds and three-quarters, and the others were almost as heavy.

On our way back to the camp we found the portage beset by innumerable and bloodthirsty foes. There are four grades of insect malignity in the woods. The mildest is represented by the winged idiot that John Burroughs' little boy called a "blunderhead." He dances stupidly before your face, as if lost in admiration, and finishes his pointless tale by getting in your eye, or down your throat. The next grade is represented by the midges. "Bite 'em no see 'em," is the Indian name for these invisible atoms of animated pepper which settle upon you in the twilight and make your skin burn like fire. But their hour is brief, and when they depart they leave not a bump behind. One step lower in the scale we find the mosquito, or rather he finds us, and makes his poisoned mark upon our skin. But after all, he has his good qualities. The mosquito is a gentlemanly pirate. He carries his weapon openly, and gives notice of an attack. He respects the decencies of life, and does not strike below the belt, or creep down the back of your neck. But the black fly is at the bottom of the moral scale. He is an unmitigated ruffian, the plug-ugly of the woods. He looks like a tiny, immature house-fly, with white legs as if he must be innocent. But, in fact, he crawls like a serpent and bites like a dog. No portion of the human frame is sacred from his greed. He takes his pound of flesh anywhere, and does not scruple to take the blood with it. As a rule you can defend yourself, to some degree, against him, by wearing a head-net, tying your sleeves around your wrists and your trousers around your ankles, and anointing yourself with grease, flavoured with pennyroyal, for which cleanly and honest scent he has a coarse aversion. But sometimes, especially on burned land, about the middle of a warm afternoon, when a rain is threatening, the horde of black flies descend in force and fury knowing that their time is short. Then there is no escape. Suits of chain armour, Nubian ointments of far-smelling potency, would not save you. You must do as our guides did on the portage, submit to fate and walk along in heroic silence, like Marco Bozzaris "bleeding at every pore,"--or do as Damon and I did, break into ejaculations and a run, until you reach a place where you can light a smudge and hold your head over it.

"And yet," said my comrade, as we sat coughing and rubbing our eyes in the painful shelter of the smoke, "there are worse trials than this in the civilised districts: social enmities, and newspaper scandals, and religious persecutions. The blackest fly I ever saw is the Reverend -----" but here his voice was fortunately choked by a fit of coughing.

A couple of wandering Indians--descendants of the Montagnais, on whose hunting domain we were travelling--dropped in at our camp that night as we sat around the fire. They gave us the latest news about the portages on our further journey; how far they had been blocked with fallen trees, and whether the water was high or low in the rivers--just as a visitor at home would talk about the effect of the strikes on the stock market, and the prospects of the newest organization of the non-voting classes for the overthrow of Tammany Hall. Every phase of civilisation or barbarism creates its own conversational currency. The weather, like the old Spanish dollar, is the only coin that passes everywhere.

But our Indians did not carry much small change about them. They were dark, silent chaps, soon talked out; and then they sat sucking their pipes before the fire, (as dumb as their own wooden effigies in front of a tobacconist's shop,) until the spirit moved them, and they vanished in their canoe down the dark lake. Our own guides were very different. They were as full of conversation as a spruce-tree is of gum. When all shallower themes were exhausted they would discourse of bears and canoes and lumber and fish, forever. After Damon and I had left the fire and rolled ourselves in the blankets in our own tent, we could hear the men going on and on with their simple jests and endless tales of adventure, until sleep drowned their voices.

It was the sound of a French chanson that woke us early on the morning of our departure from the Lake of the Bear. A gang of lumbermen were bringing a lot of logs through the lake. Half- hidden in the cold gray mist that usually betokens a fine day, and wet to the waist from splashing about after their unwieldy flock, these rough fellows were singing at their work as cheerfully as a party of robins in a cherry-tree at sunrise. It was like the miller and the two girls whom Wordsworth saw dancing in their boats on the Thames:

"They dance not for me, Yet mine is their glee! Thus pleasure is spread through the earth In stray gifts to be claimed by whoever shall find; Thus a rich loving-kindness, redundantly kind, Moves all nature to gladness and mirth."

But our later thoughts of the lumbermen were not altogether grateful, when we arrived that day, after a mile of portage, at the little Riviere Blanche, upon which we had counted to float us down to Lac Tchitagama, and found that they had stolen all its water to float their logs down the Lake of the Bear. The poor little river was as dry as a theological novel. There was nothing left of it except the bed and the bones; it was like a Connecticut stream in the middle of August. All its pretty secrets were laid bare; all its music was hushed. The pools that lingered among the rocks seemed like big tears; and the voice of the forlorn rivulets that trickled in here and there, seeking the parent stream, was a voice of weeping and complaint.

For us the loss meant a hard day's work, scrambling over slippery stones, and splashing through puddles, and forcing a way through the tangled thickets on the bank, instead of a pleasant two hours' run on a swift current. We ate our dinner on a sandbank in what was once the middle of a pretty pond; and entered, as the sun was sinking, a narrow wooded gorge between the hills, completely filled by a chain of small lakes, where travelling became easy and pleasant. The steep shores, clothed with cedar and black spruce and dark-blue fir-trees, rose sheer from the water; the passage from lake to lake was a tiny rapid a few yards long, gurgling through mossy rocks; at the foot of the chain there was a longer rapid, with a portage beside it. We emerged from the dense bush suddenly and found ourselves face to face with Lake Tchitagama.

How the heart expands at such a view! Nine miles of shining water lay stretched before us, opening through the mountains that guarded it on both sides with lofty walls of green and gray, ridge over ridge, point beyond point, until the vista ended in

"You orange sunset waning slow."

At a moment like this one feels a sense of exultation. It is a new discovery of the joy of living. And yet, my friend and I confessed to each other, there was a tinge of sadness, an inexplicable regret mingled with our joy. Was it the thought of how few human eyes had even seen that lovely vision? Was it the dim foreboding that we might never see it again? Who can explain the secret pathos of Nature's loveliness? It is a touch of melancholy inherited from our mother Eve. It is an unconscious memory of the lost Paradise. It is the sense that even if we should find another Eden, we would not be fit to enjoy it perfectly, nor stay in it forever.

Our first camp on Tchitagama was at the sunrise end of the lake, in a bay paved with small round stones, laid close together and beaten firmly down by the waves. There, and along the shores below, at the mouth of a little river that foamed in over a ledge of granite, and in the shadow of cliffs of limestone and feldspar, we trolled and took many fish: pike of enormous size, fresh-water sharks, devourers of nobler game, fit only to kill and throw away; huge old trout of six or seven pounds, with broad tails and hooked jaws, fine fighters and poor food; stupid, wide-mouthed chub--ouitouche, the Indians call them--biting at hooks that were not baited for them; and best of all, high-bred onananiche, pleasant to capture and delicate to eat.

Our second camp was on a sandy point at the sunset end of the lake-- a fine place for bathing, and convenient to the wild meadows and blueberry patches, where Damon went to hunt for bears. He did not find any; but once he heard a great noise in the bushes, which he thought was a bear; and he declared that he got quite as much excitement out of it as if it had had four legs and a mouthful of teeth.

He brought back from one of his expeditions an Indian letter, which he had found in a cleft stick by the river. It was a sheet of birch-bark with a picture drawn on it in charcoal; five Indians in a canoe paddling up the river, and one in another canoe pointing in another direction; we read it as a message left by a hunting party, telling their companions not to go on up the river, because it was already occupied, but to turn off on a side stream.

There was a sign of a different kind nailed to an old stump behind our camp. It was the top of a soap-box, with an inscription after this fashion:

A.D. MEYER & B. LEVIT Soap Mfrs. N. Y. CAMPED HERE JULY 18-- 1 TROUT 17 1/2 POUNDS. II OUAN ANISHES 18 1/2 POUNDS. ONE PIKE 147 1/2 LBS.

There was a combination of piscatorial pride and mercantile enterprise in this quaint device, that took our fancy. It suggested also a curious question of psychology in regard to the inhibitory influence of horses and fish upon the human nerve of veracity. We named the place "Point Ananias."

And yet, in fact, it was a wild and lonely spot, and not even the Hebrew inscription could spoil the sense of solitude that surrounded us when the night came, and the storm howled across the take, and the darkness encircled us with a wall that only seemed the more dense and impenetrable as the firelight blazed and leaped within the black ring.

"How far away is the nearest house, Johnny?"

"I don't know; fifty miles, I suppose."

"And what would you do if the canoes were burned, or if a tree fell and smashed them?"

"Well, I'd say a Pater noster, and take bread and bacon enough for four days, and an axe, and plenty of matches, and make a straight line through the woods. But it wouldn't be a joke, M'sieu', I can tell you."

The river Peribonca, into which Lake Tchitagama flows without a break, is the noblest of all the streams that empty into Lake St. John. It is said to be more than three hundred miles long, and at the mouth of the lake it is perhaps a thousand feet wide, flowing with a deep, still current through the forest. The dead-water lasted for several miles; then the river sloped into a rapid, spread through a net of islands, and broke over a ledge in a cataract. Another quiet stretch was followed by another fall, and so on, along the whole course of the river.

We passed three of these falls in the first day's voyage (by portages so steep and rough that an Adirondack guide would have turned gray at the sight of them), and camped at night just below the Chute du Diable, where we found some ouananiche in the foam. Our tents were on an islet, and all around we saw the primeval, savage beauty of a world unmarred by man,

The river leaped, shouting, down its double stairway of granite, rejoicing like a strong man to run a race. The after-glow in the western sky deepened from saffron to violet among the tops of the cedars, and over the cliffs rose the moonlight, paling the heavens but glorifying the earth. There was something large and generous and untrammelled in the scene, recalling one of Walt Whitman's rhapsodies:--

"Earth of departed sunsets! Earth of the mountains misty-topped! Earth of the vitreous pour of the full moon just tinged with blue! Earth of shine and dark, mottling the tide of the river!"

All the next day we went down with the current. Regiments of black spruce stood in endless files like grenadiers, each tree capped with a thick tuft of matted cones and branches. Tall white birches leaned out over the stream, Narcissus-like, as if to see their own beauty in the moving mirror. There were touches of colour on the banks, the ragged pink flowers of the Joe-Pye-weed (which always reminds me of a happy, good-natured tramp), and the yellow ear- drops of the jewel-weed, and the intense blue of the closed gentian, that strange flower which, like a reticent heart, never opens to the light. Sometimes the river spread out like a lake, between high bluffs of sand fully a mile apart; and again it divided into many channels, winding cunningly down among the islands as if it were resolved to slip around the next barrier of rock without a fall. There were eight of these huge natural dams in the course of that day's journey. Sometimes we followed one of the side canals, and made the portage at a distance from the main cataract; and sometimes we ran with the central current to the very brink of the chute, darting aside just in time to escape going over. At the foot of the last fall we made our camp on a curving beach of sand, and spent the rest of the afternoon in fishing.

It was interesting to see how closely the guides could guess at the weight of the fish by looking at them. The ouananiche are much longer in proportion to their weight than trout, and a novice almost always overestimates them. But the guides were not deceived. "This one will weigh four pounds and three-quarters, and this one four pounds, but that one not more than three pounds; he is meagre, M'sieu', BUT he is meagre." When we went ashore and tried the spring balance (which every angler ought to carry with him, as an aid to his conscience), the guides guess usually proved to be within an ounce or two of the fact. Any one of the senses can be educated to do the work of the others. The eyes of these experienced fishermen were as sensitive to weight as if they had been made to use as scales.

Below the last fall the Peribonca flows for a score of miles with an unbroken, ever-widening stream, through low shores of forest and bush and meadow. Near its mouth the Little Peribonca joins it, and the immense flood, nearly two miles wide, pours into Lake St. John. Here we saw the first outpost of civilisation--a huge unpainted storehouse, where supplies are kept for the lumbermen and the new settlers. Here also we found the tiny, lame steam launch that was to carry us back to the Hotel Roberval. Our canoes were stowed upon the roof of the cabin, and we embarked for the last stage of our long journey.

As we came out of the river-mouth, the opposite shore of the lake was invisible, and a stiff "Nor'wester" was rolling big waves across the bar. It was like putting out into the open sea. The launch laboured and puffed along for four or five miles, growing more and more asthmatic with every breath. Then there was an explosion in the engine-room. Some necessary part of the intestinal machinery had blown out. There was a moment of confusion. The captain hurried to drop the anchor, and the narrow craft lay rolling in the billows.

What to do? The captain shrugged his shoulders like a Frenchman. "Wait here, I suppose." But how long? "Who knows? Perhaps till to-morrow; perhaps the day after. They will send another boat to look for us in the course of time."

But the quarters were cramped; the weather looked ugly; if the wind should rise, the cranky launch would not be a safe cradle for the night. Damon and I preferred the canoes, for they at least would float if they were capsized. So we stepped into the frail, buoyant shells of bark once more, and danced over the big waves toward the shore. We made a camp on a wind-swept point of sand, and felt like shipwrecked mariners. But it was a gilt-edged shipwreck. For our larder was still full, and as if to provide us with the luxuries as well as the necessities of life, Nature had spread an inexhaustible dessert of the largest and most luscious blueberries around our tents.

After supper, strolling along the beach, we debated the best way of escape; whether to send one of our canoes around the eastern shore of the lake that night, to meet the steamer at the Island House and bring it to our rescue; or to set out the next morning, and paddle both canoes around the western end of the lake, thirty miles, to the Hotel Roberval. While we were talking, we came to a dry old birch-tree, with ragged, curling bark. "Here is a torch," cried Damon, "to throw light upon the situation." He touched a match to it, and the flames flashed up the tall trunk until it was transformed into a pillar of fire. But the sudden illumination burned out, and our counsels were wrapt again in darkness and uncertainty, when there came a great uproar of steam-whistles from the lake. They must be signalling for us. What could it mean?

We fired our guns, leaped into a canoe, leaving two of the guides to break camp, and paddled out swiftly into the night. It seemed an endless distance before we found the feeble light where the crippled launch was tossing at anchor. The captain shouted something about a larger steamboat and a raft of logs, out in the lake, a mile or two beyond. Presently we saw the lights, and the orange glow of the cabin windows. Was she coming, or going, or standing still? We paddled on as fast as we could, shouting and firing off a revolver until we had no more cartridges. We were resolved not to let that mysterious vessel escape us, and threw ourselves with energy into the novel excitement of chasing a steamboat in the dark.

Then the lights began to swing around; the throbbing of paddle- wheels grew louder and louder; she was evidently coming straight toward us. At that moment it flashed upon us that, while she had plenty of lights, we had none! We were lying, invisible, right across her track. The character of the steamboat chase was reversed. We turned and fled, as the guides say, a quatre pattes, into illimitable space, trying to get out of the way of our too powerful friend. It makes considerable difference, in the voyage of life, whether you chase the steamboat, or the steamboat chases you.

Meantime our other canoe had approached unseen. The steamer passed safely between the two boats, slackening speed as the pilot caught our loud halloo! She loomed up above us like a man-of-war, and as we climbed the ladder to the main-deck we felt that we had indeed gotten out of the wilderness. My old friend, Captain Savard, made us welcome. He had been sent out, much to his disgust, to catch a runaway boom of logs and tow it back to Roberval; it would be an all night affair; but we must take possession of his stateroom and make ourselves comfortable; he would certainly bring us to the hotel in time for breakfast. So he went off on the upper deck, and we heard him stamping about and yelling to his crew as they struggled to get their unwieldy drove of six thousand logs in motion.

All night long we assisted at the lumbermen's difficult enterprise. We heard the steamer snorting and straining at her clumsy, stubborn convoy. The hoarse shouts of the crew, disguised in a mongrel dialect which made them (perhaps fortunately) less intelligible and more forcible, mingled with our broken dreams.

But it was, in fact, a fitting close of our voyage. For what were we doing? It was the last stage of the woodman's labour. It was the gathering of a wild herd of the houses and churches and ships and bridges that grow in the forests, and bringing them into the fold of human service. I wonder how often the inhabitant of the snug Queen Anne cottage in the suburbs remembers the picturesque toil and varied hardship that it has cost to hew and drag his walls and floors and pretty peaked roofs out of the backwoods. It might enlarge his home, and make his musings by the winter fireside less commonplace, to give a kindly thought now and then to the long chain of human workers through whose hands the timber of his house has passed, since it first felt the stroke of the axe in the snow- bound winter woods, and floated, through the spring and summer, on far-off lakes and little rivers, au large.

1894.

TROUT-FISHING IN THE TRAUN

"Those who wish to forget painful thoughts do well to absent themselves for a time from the ties and objects that recall them; but we can be said only to fulfil our destiny in the place that gave us birth. I should on this account like well enough to spend the whole of my life in travelling abroad if I could anywhere borrow another life to spend afterwards at home."--WILLIAM HAZLITT: On Going a Journey.

The peculiarity of trout-fishing in the Traun is that one catches principally grayling. But in this it resembles some other pursuits which are not without their charm for minds open to the pleasures of the unexpected--for example, reading George Borrow's The Bible in Spain with a view to theological information, or going to the opening night at the Academy of Design with the intention of looking at pictures.

Moreover, there are really trout in the Traun, rari nantes in gurgite; and in some places more than in others; and all of high spirit, though few of great size. Thus the angler has his favourite problem: Given an unknown stream and two kinds of fish, the one better than the other; to find the better kind, and determine the hour at which they will rise. This is sport.

As for the little river itself, it has so many beauties that one does not think of asking whether it has any faults. Constant fulness, and crystal clearness, and refreshing coolness of living water, pale green like the jewel that is called aqua marina, flowing over beds of clean sand and bars of polished gravel, and dropping in momentary foam from rocky ledges, between banks that are shaded by groves of fir and ash and poplar, or through dense thickets of alder and willow, or across meadows of smooth verdure sloping up to quaint old-world villages--all these are features of the ideal little river.

I have spoken of these personal qualities first, because a truly moral writer ought to make more of character than of position. A good river in a bad country would be more worthy of affection than a bad river in a good country.

But the Traun has also the advantages of an excellent worldly position. For it rises all over the Salzkammergut, the summer hunting-ground of the Austrian Emperor, and flows through that most picturesque corner of his domain from end to end. Under the desolate cliffs of the Todtengebirge on the east, and below the shining ice-fields of the Dachstein on the south, and from the green alps around St. Wolfgang on the west, the translucent waters are gathered in little tarns, and shot through roaring brooks, and spread into lakes of wondrous beauty, and poured through growing streams, until at last they are all united just below the summer villa of his Kaiserly and Kingly Majesty, Francis Joseph, and flow away northward, through the rest of his game-preserve, into the Traunsee. It is an imperial playground, and such as I would consent to hunt the chamois in, if an inscrutable Providence had made me a kingly kaiser, or even a plain king or an unvarnished kaiser. But, failing this, I was perfectly content to spend a few idle days in fishing for trout and catching grayling, at such times and places as the law of the Austrian Empire allowed.

For it must be remembered that every stream in these over-civilised European countries belongs to somebody, by purchase or rent. And all the fish in the stream are supposed to belong to the person who owns or rents it. They do not know their master's voice, neither will they follow when he calls. But they are theoretically his. To this legal fiction the untutored American must conform. He must learn to clothe his natural desires in the raiment of lawful sanction, and take out some kind of a license before he follows his impulse to fish.

It was in the town of Aussee, at the junction of the two highest branches of the Traun, that this impulse came upon me, mildly irresistible. The full bloom of mid-July gayety in that ancient watering-place was dampened, but not extinguished, by two days of persistent and surprising showers. I had exhausted the possibilities of interest in the old Gothic church, and felt all that a man should feel in deciphering the mural tombstones of the families who were exiled for their faith in the days of the Reformation. The throngs of merry Hebrews from Vienna and Buda- Pesth, amazingly arrayed as mountaineers and milk-maids, walking up and down the narrow streets under umbrellas, had Cleopatra's charm of an infinite variety; but custom staled it. The woodland paths, winding everywhere through the plantations of fir-trees and provided with appropriate names on wooden labels, and benches for rest and conversation at discreet intervals, were too moist for even the nymphs to take delight in them. The only creatures that suffered nothing by the rain were the two swift, limpid Trauns, racing through the woods, like eager and unabashed lovers, to meet in the middle of the village. They were as clear, as joyous, as musical as if the sun were shining. The very sight of their opalescent rapids and eddying pools was an invitation to that gentle sport which is said to have the merit of growing better as the weather grows worse.

I laid this fact before the landlord of the hotel of the Erzherzog Johann, as poetically as I could, but he assured me that it was of no consequence without an invitation from the gentleman to whom the streams belonged; and he had gone away for a week. The landlord was such a good-natured person, and such an excellent sleeper, that it was impossible to believe that he could have even the smallest inaccuracy upon his conscience. So I bade him farewell, and took my way, four miles through the woods, to the lake from which one of the streams flowed.

It was called the Grundlsee. As I do not know the origin of the name, I cannot consistently make any moral or historical reflections upon it. But if it has never become famous, it ought to be, for the sake of a cozy and busy little Inn, perched on a green hill beside the lake and overlooking the whole length of it, from the groups of toy villas at the foot to the heaps of real mountains at the head. This Inn kept a thin but happy landlord, who provided me with a blue license to angle, for the inconsiderable sum of fifteen cents a day. This conferred the right of fishing not only in the Grundlsee, but also in the smaller tarn of Toplitz, a mile above it, and in the swift stream which unites them. It all coincided with my desire as if by magic. A row of a couple of miles to the head of the lake, and a walk through the forest, brought me to the smaller pond; and as the afternoon sun was ploughing pale furrows through the showers, I waded out on a point of reeds and cast the artful fly in the shadow of the great cliffs of the Dead Mountains.

It was a fit scene for a lone fisherman. But four sociable tourists promptly appeared to act as spectators and critics. Fly- fishing usually strikes the German mind as an eccentricity which calls for remonstrance. After one of the tourists had suggestively narrated the tale of seven trout which he had caught in another lake, WITH WORMS, on the previous Sunday, they went away for a row, (with salutations in which politeness but thinly veiled their pity,) and left me still whipping the water in vain. Nor was the fortune of the day much better in the stream below. It was a long and wet wade for three fish too small to keep. I came out on the shore of the lake, where I had left the row-boat, with empty bag and a feeling of damp discouragement.

There was still an hour or so of daylight, and a beautiful place to fish where the stream poured swirling out into the lake. A rise, and a large one, though rather slow, awakened my hopes. Another rise, evidently made by a heavy fish, made me certain that virtue was about to be rewarded. The third time the hook went home. I felt the solid weight of the fish against the spring of the rod, and that curious thrill which runs up the line and down the arm, changing, somehow or other, into a pleasurable sensation of excitement as it reaches the brain. But it was only for a moment; and then came that foolish, feeble shaking of the line from side to side which tells the angler that he has hooked a great, big, leather-mouthed chub--a fish which Izaak Walton says "the French esteem so mean as to call him Un Vilain." Was it for this that I had come to the country of Francis Joseph?

I took off the flies and put on one of those phantom minnows which have immortalised the name of a certain Mr. Brown. The minnow swung on a long line as the boat passed back and forth across the current, once, twice, three times-- and on the fourth circle there was a sharp strike. The rod bent almost double, and the reel sang shrilly to the first rush of the fish. He ran; he doubled; he went to the bottom and sulked; he tried to go under the boat; he did all that a game fish can do, except leaping. After twenty minutes he was tired enough to be lifted gently into the boat by a hand slipped around his gills, and there he was, a lachsforelle of three pounds' weight: small pointed head; silver sides mottled with dark spots; square, powerful tail and large fins--a fish not unlike the land-locked salmon of the Saguenay, but more delicate.

Half an hour later he was lying on the grass in front of the Inn. The waiters paused, with their hands full of dishes, to look at him; and the landlord called his guests, including my didactic tourists, to observe the superiority of the trout of the Grundlsee. The maids also came to look; and the buxom cook, with her spotless apron and bare arms akimbo, was drawn from her kitchen, and pledged her culinary honour that such a pracht-kerl should be served up in her very best style. The angler who is insensible to this sort of indirect flattery through his fish does not exist. Even the most indifferent of men thinks more favourably of people who know a good trout when they see it, and sits down to his supper with kindly feelings. Possibly he reflects, also, upon the incident as a hint of the usual size of the fish in that neighbourhood. He remembers that he may have been favoured in this case beyond his deserts by good-fortune, and resolving not to put too heavy a strain upon it, considers the next place where it would be well for him to angle.

Hallstatt is about ten miles below Aussee. The Traun here expands into a lake, very dark and deep, shut in by steep and lofty mountains. The railway runs along the eastern shore. On the other side, a mile away, you see the old town, its white houses clinging to the cliff like lichens to the face of a rock. The guide-book calls it "a highly original situation." But this is one of the cases where a little less originality and a little more reasonableness might be desired, at least by the permanent inhabitants. A ledge under the shadow of a precipice makes a trying winter residence. The people of Hallstatt are not a blooming race: one sees many dwarfs and cripples among them. But to the summer traveller the place seems wonderfully picturesque. Most of the streets are flights of steps. The high-road has barely room to edge itself through among the old houses, between the window-gardens of bright flowers. On the hottest July day the afternoon is cool and shady. The gay, little skiffs and long, open gondolas are flitting continually along the lake, which is the main street of Hallstatt.

The incongruous, but comfortable, modern hotel has a huge glass veranda, where you can eat your dinner and observe human nature in its transparent holiday disguises. I was much pleased and entertained by a family, or confederacy, of people attired as peasants--the men with feathered hats, green stockings, and bare knees--the women with bright skirts, bodices, and silk neckerchiefs--who were always in evidence, rowing gondolas with clumsy oars, meeting the steamboat at the wharf several times a day, and filling the miniature garden of the hotel with rustic greetings and early Salzkammergut attitudes. After much conjecture, I learned that they were the family and friends of a newspaper editor from Vienna. They had the literary instinct for local colour.

The fishing at Hallstatt is at Obertraun. There is a level stretch of land above the lake, where the river flows peaceably, and the fish have leisure to feed and grow. It is leased to a peasant, who makes a business of supplying the hotels with fish. He was quite willing to give permission to an angler; and I engaged one of his sons, a capital young fellow, whose natural capacities for good fellowship were only hampered by a most extraordinary German dialect, to row me across the lake, and carry the net and a small green barrel full of water to keep the fish alive, according to the custom of the country. The first day we had only four trout large enough to put into the barrel; the next day I think there were six; the third day, I remember very well, there were ten. They were pretty creatures, weighing from half a pound to a pound each, and coloured as daintily as bits of French silk, in silver gray with faint pink spots.

There was plenty to do at Hallstatt in the mornings. An hour's walk from the town there was a fine waterfall, three hundred feet high. On the side of the mountain above the lake was one of the salt-mines for which the region is celebrated. It has been worked for ages by many successive races, from the Celt downward. Perhaps even the men of the Stone Age knew of it, and came hither for seasoning to make the flesh of the cave-bear and the mammoth more palatable. Modern pilgrims are permitted to explore the long, wet, glittering galleries with a guide, and slide down the smooth wooden rollers which join the different levels of the mines. This pastime has the same fascination as sliding down the balusters; and it is said that even queens and princesses have been delighted with it. This is a touching proof of the fundamental simplicity and unity of our human nature.

But by far the best excursion from Hallstatt was an all-day trip to the Zwieselalp--a mountain which seems to have been especially created as a point of view. From the bare summit you look right into the face of the huge, snowy Dachstein, with the wild lake of Gosau gleaming at its foot; and far away on the other side your vision ranges over a confusion of mountains, with all the white peaks of the Tyrol stretched along the horizon. Such a wide outlook as this helps the fisherman to enjoy the narrow beauties of his little rivers. No sport is at its best without interruption and contrast. To appreciate wading, one ought to climb a little on odd days.

Isehl is about ten or twelve miles below Hallstatt, in the valley of the Traun. It is the fashionable summer-resort of Austria. I found it in the high tide of amusement. The shady esplanade along the river was crowded with brave women and fair men, in gorgeous raiment; the hotels were overflowing; and there were various kinds of music and entertainments at all hours of day and night. But all this did not seem to affect the fishing.

The landlord of the Konigin Elizabeth, who is also the Burgomaster and a gentleman of varied accomplishments and no leisure, kindly furnished me with a fishing license in the shape of a large pink card. There were many rules printed upon it: "All fishes under nine inches must be gently restored to the water. No instrument of capture must be used except the angle in the hand. The card of legitimation must be produced and exhibited at the polite request of any of the keepers of the river." Thus duly authorised and instructed, I sallied forth to seek my pastime according to the law.

The easiest way, in theory, was to take the afternoon train up the river to one of the villages, and fish down a mile or two in the evening, returning by the eight o'clock train. But in practice the habits of the fish interfered seriously with the latter part of this plan.

On my first day I had spent several hours in the vain effort to catch something better than small grayling. The best time for the trout was just approaching, as the broad light faded from the stream; already they were beginning to feed, when I looked up from the edge of a pool and saw the train rattling down the valley below me. Under the circumstances the only thing to do was to go on fishing. It was an even pool with steep banks, and the water ran through it very straight and swift, some four feet deep and thirty yards across. As the tail-fly reached the middle of the water, a fine trout literally turned a somersault over it, but without touching it. At the next cast he was ready, taking it with a rush that carried him into the air with the fly in his mouth. He weighed three-quarters of a pound. The next one was equally eager in rising and sharp in playing, and the third might have been his twin sister or brother. So, after casting for hours and taking nothing in the most beautiful pools, I landed three trout from one unlikely place in fifteen minutes. That was because the trout's supper-time had arrived. So had mine. I walked over to the rambling old inn at Goisern, sought the cook in the kitchen and persuaded her, in spite of the lateness of the hour, to boil the largest of the fish for my supper, after which I rode peacefully back to Ischl by the eleven o'clock train.

For the future I resolved to give up the illusory idea of coming home by rail, and ordered a little one-horse carriage to meet me at some point on the high-road every evening at nine o'clock. In this way I managed to cover the whole stream, taking a lower part each day, from the lake of Hallstatt down to Ischl.

There was one part of the river, near Laufen, where the current was very strong and waterfally, broken by ledges of rock. Below these it rested in long, smooth reaches, much beloved by the grayling. There was no difficulty in getting two or three of them out of each run.

The grayling has a quaint beauty. His appearance is aesthetic, like a fish in a pre-raphaelite picture. His colour, in midsummer, is a golden gray, darker on the back, and with a few black spots just behind his gills, like patches put on to bring out the pallor of his complexion. He smells of wild thyme when he first comes out of the water, wherefore St. Ambrose of Milan complimented him in courtly fashion "Quid specie tua gratius? Quid odore fragrantius? Quod mella fragrant, hoc tuo corpore spiras." But the chief glory of the grayling is the large iridescent fin on his back. You see it cutting the water as he swims near the surface; and when you have him on the bank it arches over him like a rainbow. His mouth is under his chin, and he takes the fly gently, by suction. He is, in fact, and to speak plainly, something of a sucker; but then he is a sucker idealised and refined, the flower of the family. Charles Cotton, the ingenious young friend of Walton, was all wrong in calling the grayling "one of the deadest-hearted fishes in the world." He fights and leaps and whirls, and brings his big fin to bear across the force of the current with a variety of tactics that would put his more aristocratic fellow-citizen, the trout, to the blush. Twelve of these pretty fellows, with a brace of good trout for the top, filled my big creel to the brim. And yet, such is the inborn hypocrisy of the human heart that I always pretended to myself to be disappointed because there were not more trout, and made light of the grayling as a thing of naught.

The pink fishing license did not seem to be of much use. Its exhibition was demanded only twice. Once a river guardian, who was walking down the stream with a Belgian Baron and encouraging him to continue fishing, climbed out to me on the end of a long embankment, and with proper apologies begged to be favoured with a view of my document. It turned out that his request was a favour to me, for it discovered the fact that I had left my fly-book, with the pink card in it, beside an old mill, a quarter of a mile up the stream.

Another time I was sitting beside the road, trying to get out of a very long, wet, awkward pair of wading-stockings, an occupation which is unfavourable to tranquillity of mind, when a man came up to me in the dusk and accosted me with an absence of politeness which in German amounted to an insult.

"Have you been fishing?"

"Why do you want to know?"

"Have you any right to fish?"

"What right have you to ask?"

"I am a keeper of the river. Where is your card?"

"It is in my pocket. But pardon my curiosity, where is YOUR card?"

This question appeared to paralyse him. He had probably never been asked for his card before. He went lumbering off in the darkness, muttering "My card? Unheard of! MY card!"

The routine of angling at Ischl was varied by an excursion to the Lake of St. Wolfgang and the Schafberg, an isolated mountain on whose rocky horn an inn has been built. It stands up almost like a bird-house on a pole, and commands a superb prospect; northward, across the rolling plain and the Bavarian forest; southward, over a tumultuous land of peaks and precipices. There are many lovely lakes in sight; but the loveliest of all is that which takes its name from the old saint who wandered hither from the country of the "furious Franks" and built his peaceful hermitage on the Falkenstein. What good taste some of those old saints had!

There is a venerable church in the village, with pictures attributed to Michael Wohlgemuth, and a chapel which is said to mark the spot where St. Wolfgang, who had lost his axe far up the mountain, found it, like Longfellow's arrow, in an oak, and "still unbroke." The tree is gone, so it was impossible to verify the story. But the saint's well is there, in a pavilion, with a bronze image over it, and a profitable inscription to the effect that the poorer pilgrims, "who have come unprovided with either money or wine, should be jolly well contented to find the water so fine." There is also a famous echo farther up the lake, which repeats six syllables with accuracy. It is a strange coincidence that there are just six syllables in the name of "der heilige Wolfgang." But when you translate it into English, the inspiration of the echo seems to be less exact. The sweetest thing about St. Wolfgang was the abundance of purple cyclamens, clothing the mountain meadows, and filling the air with delicate fragrance like the smell of lilacs around a New England farmhouse in early June.

There was still one stretch of the river above Ischl left for the last evening's sport. I remember it so well: the long, deep place where the water ran beside an embankment of stone, and the big grayling poised on the edge of the shadow, rising and falling on the current as a kite rises and falls on the wind and balances back to the same position; the murmur of the stream and the hissing of the pebbles underfoot in the rapids as the swift water rolled them over and over; the odour of the fir-trees, and the streaks of warm air in quiet places, and the faint whiffs of wood-smoke wafted from the houses, and the brown flies dancing heavily up and down in the twilight; the last good pool, where the river was divided, the main part making a deep, narrow curve to the right, and the lesser part bubbling into it over a bed of stones with half-a-dozen tiny waterfalls, with a fine trout lying at the foot of each of them and rising merrily as the white fly passed over him--surely it was all very good, and a memory to be grateful for. And when the basket was full, it was pleasant to put off the heavy wading-shoes and the long rubber-stockings, and ride homeward in an open carriage through the fresh night air. That is as near to sybaritic luxury as a man should care to come.

The lights in the cottages are twinkling like fire-flies, and there are small groups of people singing and laughing down the road. The honest fisherman reflects that this world is only a place of pilgrimage, but after all there is a good deal of cheer on the journey, if it is made with a contented heart. He wonders who the dwellers in the scattered houses may be, and weaves romances out of the shadows on the curtained windows. The lamps burning in the wayside shrines tell him stories of human love and patience and hope, and of divine forgiveness. Dream-pictures of life float before him, tender and luminous, filled with a vague, soft atmosphere in which the simplest outlines gain a strange significance. They are like some of Millet's paintings--"The

Sower," or "The Sheepfold,"--there is very little detail in them but sometimes a little means so much.

Then the moon slips up into the sky from behind the hills, and the fisherman begins to think of home, and of the foolish, fond old rhymes about those whom the moon sees far away, and the stars that have the power to fulfil wishes--as if the celestial bodies knew or cared anything about our small nerve-thrills which we call affection and desires! But if there were Some One above the moon and stars who did know and care, Some One who could see the places and the people that you and I would give so much to see, Some One who could do for them all of kindness that you and I fain would do, Some One able to keep our beloved in perfect peace and watch over the little children sleeping in their beds beyond the sea--what then? Why, then, in the evening hour, one might have thoughts of home that would go across the ocean by way of heaven, and be better than dreams, almost as good as prayers.

AT THE SIGN OF THE BALSAM BOUGH

"Come live with me, and be my love, And we will all the pleasures prove That valleys, groves, or hills, or field, Or woods and steepy mountains yield.

"There we will rest our sleepy heads, And happy hearts, on balsam beds; And every day go forth to fish In foamy streams for ouananiche."

Old Song with a new Ending.

It has been asserted, on high philosophical authority, that woman is a problem. She is more; she is a cause of problems to others. This is not a theoretical statement. It is a fact of experience.

Every year, when the sun passes the summer solstice, the

"Two souls with but a single thought,"

of whom I am so fortunate as to be one, are summoned by that portion of our united mind which has at once the right of putting the question and of casting the deciding vote, to answer this conundrum: How can we go abroad without crossing the ocean, and abandon an interesting family of children without getting completely beyond their reach, and escape from the frying-pan of housekeeping without falling into the fire of the summer hotel? This apparently insoluble problem we usually solve by going to camp in Canada.

It is indeed a foreign air that breathes around us as we make the harmless, friendly voyage from Point Levis to Quebec. The boy on the ferry-boat, who cajoles us into buying a copy of Le Moniteur containing last month's news, has the address of a true though diminutive Frenchman. The landlord of the quiet little inn on the outskirts of the town welcomes us with Gallic effusion as well- known guests, and rubs his hands genially before us, while he escorts us to our apartments, groping secretly in his memory to recall our names. When we walk down the steep, quaint streets to revel in the purchase of moccasins and water-proof coats and camping supplies, we read on a wall the familiar but transformed legend, L'enfant pleurs, il veut son Camphoria, and remember with joy that no infant who weeps in French can impose any responsibility upon us in these days of our renewed honeymoon.

But the true delight of the expedition begins when the tents have been set up, in the forest back of Lake St. John, and the green branches have been broken for the woodland bed, and the fire has been lit under the open sky, and, the livery of fashion being all discarded, I sit down at a log table to eat supper with my lady Greygown. Then life seems simple and amiable and well worth living. Then the uproar and confusion of the world die away from us, and we hear only the steady murmur of the river and the low voice of the wind in the tree-tops. Then time is long, and the only art that is needful for its enjoyment is short and easy. Then we taste true comfort, while we lodge with Mother Green at the Sign of the Balsam Bough.

I.

UNDER THE WHITE BIRCHES.

Men may say what they will in praise of their houses, and grow eloquent upon the merits of various styles of architecture, but, for our part, we are agreed that there is nothing to be compared with a tent. It is the most venerable and aristocratic form of human habitation. Abraham and Sarah lived in it, and shared its hospitality with angels. It is exempt from the base tyranny of the plumber, the paper-hanger, and the gas-man. It is not immovably bound to one dull spot of earth by the chains of a cellar and a system of water-pipes. It has a noble freedom of locomotion. It follows the wishes of its inhabitants, and goes with them, a travelling home, as the spirit moves them to explore the wilderness. At their pleasure, new beds of wild flowers surround it, new plantations of trees overshadow it, and new avenues of shining water lead to its ever-open door. What the tent lacks in luxury it makes up in liberty: or rather let us say that liberty itself is the greatest luxury.

Another thing is worth remembering--a family which lives in a tent never can have a skeleton in the closet.

But it must not be supposed that every spot in the woods is suitable for a camp, or that a good tenting-ground can be chosen without knowledge and forethought. One of the requisites, indeed, is to be found everywhere in the St. John region; for all the lakes and rivers are full of clear, cool water, and the traveller does not need to search for a spring. But it is always necessary to look carefully for a bit of smooth ground on the shore, far enough above the water to be dry, and slightly sloping, so that the head of the bed may be higher than the foot. Above all, it must be free from big stones and serpentine roots of trees. A root that looks no bigger that an inch-worm in the daytime assumes the proportions of a boa-constrictor at midnight--when you find it under your hip- bone. There should also be plenty of evergreens near at hand for the beds. Spruce will answer at a pinch; it has an aromatic smell; but it is too stiff and humpy. Hemlock is smoother and more flexible; but the spring soon wears out of it. The balsam-fir, with its elastic branches and thick flat needles, is the best of all. A bed of these boughs a foot deep is softer than a mattress and as fragrant as a thousand Christmas-trees. Two things more are needed for the ideal camp-ground--an open situation, where the breeze will drive away the flies and mosquitoes, and an abundance of dry firewood within easy reach. Yes, and a third thing must not be forgotten; for, says my lady Greygown:

"I shouldn't feel at home in camp unless I could sit in the door of the tent and look out across flowing water."

All these conditions are met in our favourite camping place below the first fall in the Grande Decharge. A rocky point juts out into the rivet and makes a fine landing for the canoes. There is a dismantled fishing-cabin a few rods back in the woods, from which we can borrow boards for a table and chairs. A group of cedars on the lower edge of the point opens just wide enough to receive and shelter our tent. At a good distance beyond ours, the guides' tent is pitched; and the big camp-fire burns between the two dwellings. A pair of white-birches lift their leafy crowns far above us, and after them we name the place Le Camp aux Bouleaux.

"Why not call trees people?--since, if you come to live among them year after year, you will learn to know many of them personally, and an attachment will grow up between you and them individually." So writes that Doctor Amabilis of woodcraft, W. C. Prime, in his book, Among the Northern Hills, and straightway launches forth into eulogy on the white-birch. And truly it is an admirable, lovable, and comfortable tree, beautiful to look upon and full of various uses. Its wood is strong to make paddles and axe handles, and glorious to burn, blazing up at first with a flashing flame, and then holding the fire in its glowing heart all through the night. Its bark is the most serviceable of all the products of the wilderness. In Russia, they say, it is used in tanning, and gives its subtle, sacerdotal fragrance to Russia leather. But here, in the woods, it serves more primitive ends. It can be peeled off in a huge roll from some giant tree and fashioned into a swift canoe to carry man over the waters. It can be cut into square sheets to roof his shanty in the forest. It is the paper on which he writes his woodland despatches, and the flexible material which he bends into drinking-cups of silver lined with gold. A thin strip of it wrapped around the end of a candle and fastened in a cleft stick makes a practicable chandelier. A basket for berries, a horn to call the lovelorn moose through the autumnal woods, a canvas on which to draw the outline of great and memorable fish--all these and many other indispensable luxuries are stored up for the skilful woodsman in the birch bark.

Only do not rob or mar the tree, unless you really need what it has to give you. Let it stand and grow in virgin majesty, ungirdled and unscarred, while the trunk becomes a firm pillar of the forest temple, and the branches spread abroad a refuge of bright green leaves for the birds of the air. Nature never made a more excellent piece of handiwork. "And if," said my lady Greygown, "I should ever become a dryad, I would choose to be transformed into a white-birch. And then, when the days of my life were numbered, and the sap had ceased to flow, and the last leaf had fallen, and the dry bark hung around me in ragged curls and streamers, some wandering hunter would come in the wintry night and touch a lighted coal to my body, and my spirit would flash up in a fiery chariot into the sky."

The chief occupation of our idle days on the Grande Decharge was fishing. Above the camp spread a noble pool, more than two miles in circumference, and diversified with smooth bays and whirling eddies, sand beaches and rocky islands. The river poured into it at the head, foaming and raging down a long chute, and swept out of it just in front of our camp in a merry, musical rapid. It was full of fish of various kinds--long-nosed pickerel, wall-eyed pike, and stupid chub. But the prince of the pool was the fighting ouananiche, the little salmon of St. John.

Here let me chant thy praise, thou noblest and most high-minded fish, the cleanest feeder, the merriest liver, the loftiest leaper, and the bravest warrior of all creatures that swim! Thy cousin, the trout, in his purple and gold with crimson spots, wears a more splendid armour than thy russet and silver mottled with black, but thine is the kinglier nature. His courage and skill compared with thine

"Are as moonlight unto sunlight, and as water unto wine."

The old salmon of the sea who begot thee, long ago, in these inland waters, became a backslider, descending again to the ocean, and grew gross and heavy with coarse feeding. But thou, unsalted salmon of the foaming floods, not landlocked, as men call thee, but choosing of thine own free-will to dwell on a loftier level, in the pure, swift current of a living stream, hast grown in grace and risen to a higher life. Thou art not to be measured by quantity, but by quality, and thy five pounds of pure vigour will outweigh a score of pounds of flesh less vitalised by spirit. Thou feedest on the flies of the air, and thy food is transformed into an aerial passion for flight, as thou springest across the pool, vaulting toward the sky. Thine eyes have grown large and keen by peering through the foam, and the feathered hook that can deceive thee must be deftly tied and delicately cast. Thy tail and fins, by ceaseless conflict with the rapids, have broadened and strengthened, so that they can flash thy slender body like a living arrow up the fall. As Lancelot among the knights, so art thou among the fish, the plain-armoured hero, the sunburnt champion of all the water-folk.

Every morning and evening, Greygown and I would go out for ouananiche, and sometimes we caught plenty and sometimes few, but we never came back without a good catch of happiness. There were certain places where the fish liked to stay. For example, we always looked for one at the lower corner of a big rock, very close to it, where he could poise himself easily on the edge of the strong downward stream. Another likely place was a straight run of water, swift, but not too swift, with a sunken stone in the middle. The ouananiche does not like crooked, twisting water. An even current is far more comfortable, for then he discovers just how much effort is needed to balance against it, and keeps up the movement mechanically, as if he were half asleep. But his favourite place is under one of the floating islands of thick foam that gather in the corners below the falls. The matted flakes give a grateful shelter from the sun, I fancy, and almost all game-fish love to lie in the shade; but the chief reason why the onananiche haunt the drifting white mass is because it is full of flies and gnats, beaten down by the spray of the cataract, and sprinkled all through the foam like plums in a cake. To this natural confection the little salmon, lurking in his corner, plays the part of Jack Horner all day long, and never wearies.

"See that belle brou down below there!" said Ferdinand, as we scrambled over the huge rocks at the foot of the falls; "there ought to be salmon there en masse." Yes, there were the sharp noses picking out the unfortunate insects, and the broad tails waving lazily through the foam as the fish turned in the water. At this season of the year, when summer is nearly ended, and every ouananiche in the Grande Decharge has tasted feathers and seen a hook, it is useless to attempt to delude them with the large gaudy flies which the fishing-tackle-maker recommends. There are only two successful methods of angling now. The first of these I tried, and by casting delicately with a tiny brown trout-fly tied on a gossamer strand of gut, captured a pair of fish weighing about three pounds each. They fought against the spring of the four- ounce rod for nearly half an hour before Ferdinand could slip the net around them. But there was another and a broader tail still waving disdainfully on the outer edge of the foam. "And now," said the gallant Ferdinand, "the turn is to madame, that she should prove her fortune--attend but a moment, madame, while I seek the sauterelle."

This was the second method: the grasshopper was attached to the hook, and casting the line well out across the pool, Ferdinand put the rod into Greygown's hands. She stood poised upon a pinnacle of rock, like patience on a monument, waiting for a bite. It came. There was a slow, gentle pull at the line, answered by a quick jerk of the rod, and a noble fish flashed into the air. Four pounds and a half at least! He leaped again and again, shaking the drops from his silvery sides. He rushed up the rapids as if he had determined to return to the lake, and down again as if he had changed his plans and determined to go to the Saguenay. He sulked in the deep water and rubbed his nose against the rocks. He did his best to treat that treacherous grasshopper as the whale served Jonah. But Greygown, through all her little screams and shouts of excitement, was steady and sage. She never gave the fish an inch of slack line; and at last he lay glittering on the rocks, with the black St. Andrew's crosses clearly marked on his plump sides, and the iridescent spots gleaming on his small, shapely head. "Une belle!" cried Ferdinand, as he held up the fish in triumph, "and it is madame who has the good fortune. She understands well to take the large fish--is it not?" Greygown stepped demurely down from her pinnacle, and as we drifted down the pool in the canoe, under the mellow evening sky, her conversation betrayed not a trace of the pride that a victorious fisherman would have shown. On the contrary, she insisted that angling was an affair of chance-- which was consoling, though I knew it was not altogether true--and that the smaller fish were just as pleasant to catch and better to eat, after all. For a generous rival, commend me to a woman. And if I must compete, let it be with one who has the grace to dissolve the bitter of defeat in the honey of a mutual self-congratulation.

We had a garden, and our favourite path through it was the portage leading around the falls. We travelled it very frequently, making an excuse of idle errands to the steamboat-landing on the lake, and sauntering along the trail as if school were out and would never keep again. It was the season of fruits rather than of flowers. Nature was reducing the decorations of her table to make room for the banquet. She offered us berries instead of blossoms.

There were the light coral clusters of the dwarf cornel set in whorls of pointed leaves; and the deep blue bells of the Clintonia borealis (which the White Mountain people call the bear-berry, and I hope the name will stick, for it smacks of the woods, and it is a shame to leave so free and wild a plant under the burden of a Latin name); and the gray, crimson-veined berries for which the Canada Mayflower had exchanged its feathery white bloom; and the ruby drops of the twisted stalk hanging like jewels along its bending stem. On the three-leaved table which once carried the gay flower of the wake-robin, there was a scarlet lump like a red pepper escaped to the forest and run wild. The partridge-vine was full of rosy provision for the birds. The dark tiny leaves of the creeping snow-berry were all sprinkled over with delicate drops of spicy foam. There were few belated raspberries, and, if we chose to go out into the burnt ground, we could find blueberries in plenty.

But there was still bloom enough to give that festal air without which the most abundant feast seems coarse and vulgar. The pale gold of the loosestrife had faded, but the deeper yellow of the goldenrod had begun to take its place. The blue banners of the fleur-de-lis had vanished from beside the springs, but the purple of the asters was appearing. Closed gentians kept their secret inviolate, and bluebells trembled above the rocks. The quaint pinkish-white flowers of the turtle-head showed in wet places, and instead of the lilac racemes of the purple-fringed orchis, which had disappeared with midsummer, we found now the slender braided spikes of the lady's-tresses, latest and lowliest of the orchids, pale and pure as nuns of the forest, and exhaling a celestial fragrance. There is a secret pleasure in finding these delicate flowers in the rough heart of the wilderness. It is like discovering the veins of poetry in the character of a guide or a lumberman. And to be able to call the plants by name makes them a hundredfold more sweet and intimate. Naming things is one of the oldest and simplest of human pastimes. Children play at it with their dolls and toy animals. In fact, it was the first game ever played on earth, for the Creator who planted the garden eastward in Eden knew well what would please the childish heart of man, when He brought all the new-made creatures to Adam, "to see what he would call them."

Our rustic bouquet graced the table under the white-birches, while we sat by the fire and watched our four men at the work of the camp--Joseph and Raoul chopping wood in the distance; Francois slicing juicy rashers from the flitch of bacon; and Ferdinand, the chef, heating the frying-pan in preparation for supper.

"Have you ever thought," said Greygown, in a contented tone of voice, "that this is the only period of our existence when we attain to the luxury of a

French cook?"

"And one with the grand manner, too," I replied, "for he never fails to ask what it is that madame desires to eat to-day, as if the larder of Lucullus were at his disposal, though he knows well enough that the only choice lies between broiled fish and fried fish, or bacon with eggs and a rice omelet. But I like the fiction of a lordly ordering of the repast. How much better it is than having to eat what is flung before you at a summer boarding-house by a scornful waitress!"

"Another thing that pleases me," continued my lady, "is the unbreakableness of the dishes. There are no nicks in the edges of the best plates here; and, oh! it is a happy thing to have a home without bric-a-brac. There is nothing here that needs to be dusted."

"And no engagements for to-morrow," I ejaculated. "Dishes that can't be broken, and plans that can--that's the ideal of housekeeping."

"And then," added my philosopher in skirts, "it is certainly refreshing to get away from all one's relations for a little while."

"But how do you make that out?" I asked, in mild surprise. "What are you going to do with me?"

"Oh," said she, with a fine air of independence, "I don't count you. You are not a relation, only a connection by marriage."

"Well, my dear," I answered, between the meditative puffs of my pipe, "it is good to consider the advantages of our present situation. We shall soon come into the frame of mind of the Sultan of Morocco when he camped in the Vale of Rabat. The place pleased him so well that he staid until the very pegs of his tent took root and grew up into a grove of trees around his pavilion."

II.

KENOGAMI.

The guides were a little restless under the idle regime of our lazy camp, and urged us to set out upon some adventure. Ferdinand was like the uncouth swain in Lycidas. Sitting upon the bundles of camp equipage on the shore, and crying,--

"To-morrow to fresh woods and pastures new,"

he led us forth to seek the famous fishing grounds on Lake Kenogami.

We skirted the eastern end of Lake St. John in our two canoes, and pushed up La Belle Riviere to Hebertville, where all the children turned out to follow our procession through the village. It was like the train that tagged after the Pied Piper of Hamelin. We embarked again, surrounded by an admiring throng, at the bridge where the main street crossed a little stream, and paddled up it, through a score of back yards and a stretch of reedy meadows, where the wild and tame ducks fed together, tempting the sportsman to sins of ignorance. We crossed the placid Lac Vert, and after a carry of a mile along the high-road toward Chicoutimi, turned down a steep hill and pitched our tents on a crescent of silver sand, with the long, fair water of Kenogami before us.

It is amazing to see how quickly these woodsmen can make a camp. Each one knew precisely his share of the enterprise. One sprang to chop a dry spruce log into fuel for a quick fire, and fell a harder tree to keep us warm through the night. Another stripped a pile of boughs from a balsam for the beds. Another cut the tent-poles from a neighbouring thicket. Another unrolled the bundles and made ready the cooking utensils. As if by magic, the miracle of the camp was accomplished.--

"The bed was made, the room was fit, By punctual eve the stars were lit"--

but Greygown always insists upon completing that quotation from Stevenson in her own voice; for this is the way it ends,--

"When we put up, my ass and I, At God's green caravanserai."

Our permanent camp was another day's voyage down the lake, on a beach opposite the Point Ausable. There the water was contracted to a narrow strait, and in the swift current, close to the point, the great trout had fixed their spawning-bed from time immemorial. It was the first week in September, and the magnates of the lake were already assembling--the Common Councilmen and the Mayor and the whole Committee of Seventy. There were giants in that place, rolling lazily about, and chasing each other on the surface of the water. "Look, M'sieu'!" cried Francois, in excitement, as we lay at anchor in the gray morning twilight; "one like a horse has just leaped behind us; I assure you, big like a horse!"

But the fish were shy and dour. Old Castonnier, the guardian of the lake, lived in his hut on the shore, and flogged the water, early and late, every day with his home-made flies. He was anchored in his dugout close beside us, and grinned with delight as he saw his over-educated trout refuse my best casts. "They are here, M'sieu', for you can see them," he said, by way of discouragement, "but it is difficult to take them. Do you not find it so?"

In the back of my fly-book I discovered a tiny phantom minnow--a dainty affair of varnished silk, as light as a feather--and quietly attached it to the leader in place of the tail-fly. Then the fun began.

One after another the big fish dashed at that deception, and we played and netted them, until our score was thirteen, weighing altogether thirty-five pounds, and the largest five pounds and a half. The guardian was mystified and disgusted. He looked on for a while in silence, and then pulled up anchor and clattered ashore. He must have made some inquiries and reflections during the day, for that night he paid a visit to our camp. After telling bear stories and fish stories for an hour or two by the fire, he rose to depart, and tapping his forefinger solemnly upon my shoulder, delivered himself as follows:--

"You can say a proud thing when you go home, M'sieu'--that you have beaten the old Castonnier. There are not many fishermen who can say that. "But," he added, with confidential emphasis, "c'etait votre sacre p'tit poisson qui a fait cela."

That was a touch of human nature, my rusty old guardian, more welcome to me than all the morning's catch. Is there not always a "confounded little minnow" responsible for our failures? Did you ever see a school-boy tumble on the ice without stooping immediately to re-buckle the strap of his skates? And would not Ignotus have painted a masterpiece if he could have found good brushes and a proper canvas? Life's shortcomings would be bitter indeed if we could not find excuses for them outside of ourselves. And as for life's successes--well, it is certainly wholesome to remember how many of them are due to a fortunate position and the proper tools.

Our tent was on the border of a coppice of young trees. It was pleasant to be awakened by a convocation of birds at sunrise, and to watch the shadows of the leaves dance out upon our translucent roof of canvas.

All the birds in the bush are early, but there are so many of them that it is difficult to believe that every one can be rewarded with a worm. Here in Canada those little people of the air who appear as transient guests of spring and autumn in the Middle States, are in their summer home and breeding-place. Warblers, named for the magnolia and the myrtle, chestnut-sided, bay-breasted, blue-backed, and black-throated, flutter and creep along the branches with simple lisping music. Kinglets, ruby-crowned and golden-crowned, tiny, brilliant sparks of life, twitter among the trees, breaking occasionally into clearer, sweeter songs. Companies of redpolls and crossbills pass chirping through the thickets, busily seeking their food. The fearless, familiar chickadee repeats his name merrily, while he leads his family to explore every nook and cranny of the wood. Cedar wax-wings, sociable wanderers, arrive in numerous flocks. The Canadians call them "recollets," because they wear a brown crest of the same colour as the hoods of the monks who came with the first settlers to New France. They are a songless tribe, although their quick, reiterated call as they take to flight has given them the name of chatterers. The beautiful tree-sparrows and the pine-siskins are more melodious, and the slate-coloured juncos, flitting about the camp, are as garrulous as chippy-birds. All these varied notes come and go through the tangle of morning dreams. And now the noisy blue-jay is calling "Thief--thief--thief!" in the distance, and a pair of great pileated woodpeckers with crimson crests are laughing loudly in the swamp over some family joke. But listen! what is that harsh creaking note? It is the cry of the Northern shrike, of whom tradition says that he catches little birds and impales them on sharp thorns. At the sound of his voice the concert closes suddenly and the singers vanish into thin air. The hour of music is over; the commonplace of day has begun. And there is my lady Greygown, already up and dressed, standing by the breakfast-table and laughing at my belated appearance.

But the birds were not our only musicians at Kenogami. French Canada is one of the ancestral homes of song. Here you can still listen to those quaint ballads which were sung centuries ago in Normandie and Provence. "A la Claire Fontaine," "Dans Paris y a-t- une Brune plus Belle que le Jour," "Sur le Pont d'Avignon," "En Roulant ma Boule," "La Poulette Grise," and a hundred other folk- songs linger among the peasants and voyageurs of these northern woods. You may hear

"Malbrouck s'en va-t-en guerre-- Mironton, mironton, mirontaine,"

and

"Isabeau s'y promene Le long de son jardin,"

chanted in the farmhouse or the lumber shanty, to the tunes which have come down from an unknown source, and never lost their echo in the hearts of the people.

Our Ferdinand was a perfect fountain of music. He had a clear tenor voice, and solaced every task and shortened every voyage with melody. "A song, Ferdinand, a jolly song," the other men would say, as the canoes went sweeping down the quiet lake. And then the leader would strike up a well-known air, and his companions would come in on the refrain, keeping time with the stroke of their paddles. Sometimes it would be a merry ditty:

"My father had no girl but me, And yet he sent me off to sea; Leap, my little Cecilia."

Or perhaps it was:

"I've danced so much the livelong day,-- Dance, my sweetheart, let's be gay,-- I've fairly danced my shoes away,-- Till evening. Dance, my pretty, dance once more; Dance, until we break the floor."

But more frequently the song was touched with a plaintive pleasant melancholy. The minstrel told how he had gone into the woods and heard the nightingale, and she had confided to him that lovers are often unhappy. The story of La Belle Francoise was repeated in minor cadences--how her sweetheart sailed away to the wars, and when he came back the village church bells were ringing, and he said to himself that Francoise had been faithless, and the chimes were for her marriage; but when he entered the church it was her funeral that he saw, for she had died of love. It is strange how sorrow charms us when it is distant and visionary. Even when we are happiest we enjoy making music

"Of old, unhappy, far-off things."

"What is that song which you are singing, Ferdinand?" asks the lady, as she hears him humming behind her in the canoe.

"Ah, madame, it is the chanson of a young man who demands of his blonde why she will not marry him. He says that he has waited long time, and the flowers are falling from the rose-tree, and he is very sad."

"And does she give a reason?"

"Yes, madame--that is to say, a reason of a certain sort; she declares that she is not quite ready; he must wait until the rose- tree adorns itself again."

"And what is the end--do they get married at last?"

"But I do not know, madame. The chanson does not go so far. It ceases with the complaint of the young man. And it is a very uncertain affair--this affair of the heart--is it not?"

Then, as if he turned from such perplexing mysteries to something plain and sure and easy to understand, he breaks out into the jolliest of all Canadian songs:

"My bark canoe that flies, that flies, Hola! my bark canoe!"

III.

THE ISLAND POOL.

Among the mountains there is a gorge. And in the gorge there is a river. And in the river there is a pool. And in the pool there is an island. And on the island, for four happy days, there was a camp.

It was by no means an easy matter to establish ourselves in that lonely place. The river, though not remote from civilisation, is practically inaccessible for nine miles of its course by reason of the steepness of its banks, which are long, shaggy precipices, and the fury of its current, in which no boat can live. We heard its voice as we approached through the forest, and could hardly tell whether it was far away or near.

There is a perspective of sound as well as of sight, and one must have some idea of the size of a noise before one can judge of its distance. A mosquito's horn in a dark room may seem like a trumpet on the battlements; and the tumult of a mighty stream heard through an unknown stretch of woods may appear like the babble of a mountain brook close at hand.

But when we came out upon the bald forehead of a burnt cliff and looked down, we realised the grandeur and beauty of the unseen voice that we had been following. A river of splendid strength went leaping through the chasm five hundred feet below us, and at the foot of two snow-white falls, in an oval of dark topaz water, traced with curves of floating foam, lay the solitary island.

The broken path was like a ladder. "How shall we ever get down?" sighed Greygown, as we dropped from rock to rock; and at the bottom she looked up sighing, "I know we never can get back again." There was not a foot of ground on the shores level enough for a tent. Our canoe ferried us over, two at a time, to the island. It was about a hundred paces long, composed of round, coggly stones, with just one patch of smooth sand at the lower end. There was not a tree left upon it larger than an alder-bush. The tent-poles must be cut far up on the mountain-sides, and every bough for our beds must be carried down the ladder of rocks. But the men were gay at their work, singing like mocking-birds. After all, the glow of life comes from friction with its difficulties. If we cannot find them at home, we sally abroad and create them, just to warm up our mettle.

The ouananiche in the island pool were superb, astonishing, incredible. We stood on the cobble-stones at the upper end, and cast our little flies across the sweeping stream, and for three days the fish came crowding in to fill the barrel of pickled salmon for our guides' winter use; and the score rose,-- twelve, twenty- one, thirty-two; and the size of the "biggest fish" steadily mounted--four pounds, four and a half, five, five and three- quarters. "Precisely almost six pounds," said Ferdinand, holding the scales; "but we may call him six, M'sieu', for if it had been to-morrow that we had caught him, he would certainly have gained the other ounce." And yet, why should I repeat the fisherman's folly of writing down the record of that marvellous catch? We always do it, but we know that it is a vain thing. Few listen to the tale, and none accept it. Does not Christopher North, reviewing the Salmonia of Sir Humphry Davy, mock and jeer unfeignedly at the fish stories of that most reputable writer? But, on the very next page, old Christopher himself meanders on into a perilous narrative of the day when he caught a whole cart-load of trout in a Highland loch. Incorrigible, happy inconsistency! Slow to believe others, and full of sceptical inquiry, fond man never doubts one thing--that somewhere in the world a tribe of gentle readers will be discovered to whom his fish stories will appear credible.

One of our days on the island was Sunday--a day of rest in a week of idleness. We had a few books; for there are some in existence which will stand the test of being brought into close contact with nature. Are not John Burroughs' cheerful, kindly essays full of woodland truth and companionship? Can you not carry a whole library of musical philosophy in your pocket in Matthew Arnold's volume of selections from Wordsworth? And could there be a better sermon for a Sabbath in the wilderness than Mrs. Slosson's immortal story of Fishin' Jimmy?

But to be very frank about the matter, the camp is not stimulating to the studious side of my mind. Charles Lamb, as usual, has said what I feel: "I am not much a friend to out-of-doors reading. I cannot settle my spirits to it."

There are blueberries growing abundantly among the rocks--huge clusters of them, bloomy and luscious as the grapes of Eshcol. The blueberry is nature's compensation for the ruin of forest fires. It grows best where the woods have been burned away and the soil is too poor to raise another crop of trees. Surely it is an innocent and harmless pleasure to wander along the hillsides gathering these wild fruits, as the Master and His disciples once walked through the fields and plucked the ears of corn, never caring what the Pharisees thought of that new way of keeping the Sabbath.

And here is a bed of moss beside a dashing rivulet, inviting us to rest and be thankful. Hark! There is a white-throated sparrow, on a little tree across the river, whistling his afternoon song

"In linked sweetness long drawn out."

Down in Maine they call him the Peabody-bird, because his notes sound to them like Old man--Peabody, peabody, peabody. In New Brunswick the Scotch settlers say that he sings Lost--lost-- Kennedy, kennedy, kennedy. But here in his northern home I think we can understand him better. He is singing again and again, with a cadence that never wearies, "Sweet--sweet--Canada, canada, canada!" The Canadians, when they came across the sea, remembering the nightingale of southern France, baptised this little gray minstrel their rossignol, and the country ballads are full of his praise. Every land has its nightingale, if we only have the heart to hear him. How distinct his voice is--how personal, how confidential, as if he had a message for us!

There is a breath of fragrance on the cool shady air beside our little stream, that seems familiar. It is the first week of September. Can it be that the twin-flower of June, the delicate Linnaea borealis, is blooming again? Yes, here is the threadlike stem lifting its two frail pink bells above the bed of shining leaves. How dear an early flower seems when it comes back again and unfolds its beauty in a St. Martin's summer! How delicate and suggestive is the faint, magical odour! It is like a renewal of the dreams of youth.

"And need we ever grow old?" asked my lady Greygown, as she sat that evening with the twin-flower on her breast, watching the stars come out along the edge of the cliffs, and tremble on the hurrying tide of the river. "Must we grow old as well as gray? Is the time coming when all life will be commonplace and practical, and governed by a dull 'of course'? Shall we not always find adventures and romances, and a few blossoms returning, even when the season grows late?"

"At least," I answered, "let us believe in the possibility, for to doubt it is to destroy it. If we can only come back to nature together every year, and consider the flowers and the birds, and confess our faults and mistakes and our unbelief under these silent stars, and hear the river murmuring our absolution, we shall die young, even though we live long: we shall have a treasure of memories which will be like the twin-flower, always a double blossom on a single stem, and carry with us into the unseen world something which will make it worth while to be immortal."

1894.

A SONG AFTER SUNDOWN

"There's no music like a little river's. It plays the same tune (and that's the favourite) over and over again, and yet does not weary of it like men fiddlers. It takes the mind out of doors; and though we should be grateful for good houses, there is, after all, no house like god's out-of-doors. And lastly, sir, it quiets a man down like saying his prayers."--ROBERT LOUIS STEVENSON: Prince Otto.

THE WOOD-NOTES OF THE VEERY

The moonbeams over Arno's vale in silver flood were pouring, When first I heard the nightingale a long-lost love deploring: So passionate, so full of pain, it sounded strange and eerie, I longed to hear a simpler strain, the wood-notes of the veery.

The laverock sings a bonny lay, above the Scottish heather, It sprinkles from the dome of day like light and love together; He drops the golden notes to greet his brooding mate, his dearie; I only know one song more sweet, the vespers of the veery.

In English gardens green and bright, and rich in fruity treasure, I've heard the blackbird with delight repeat his merry measure; The ballad was a lively one, the tune was loud and cheery, And yet with every setting sun I listened for the veery.

O far away, and far away, the tawny thrush is singing, New England woods at close of day with that clear chant are ringing; And when my light of life is low, and heart and flesh are weary, I fain would hear, before I go, the wood-notes of the veery.

1895.

www.ingramcontent.com/pod-product-compliance
Lightning Source LLC
Chambersburg PA
CBHW071047290526
45795CB00004B/1374